D0188597

OUTLAWS
On The Big River

Joe Schwab (signature)

JOE SCHWAB

Copyright © 2010 Joe R Schwab
All rights reserved.

ISBN: 1451556365
ISBN-13: 9781451556360

Prologue

The following stories and events are all based on true happenings. Names and locations may have been altered.

No reference to commercial fishing or sport fishing is intended to denigrate the activity in any way. It is simply a recount of the many ways people abuse the resource or flout the laws designed to protect the resource.

The Columbia River runs between Oregon on the south and Washington on the north. This section of the river is subject to both commercial and sport fishing as well as the exercise of treaty Indian fishing by local tribes that have lived along the river for thousands of years.

Salmon and Steelhead runs once numbered in the millions each year, now total less than 500,00. Harvest, habitat, hydropower and hatcheries all have contributed in one way or the other to the decline of wild fish within the system.

These stories simply tell of the problems, hazards and complexities of law enforcement in its attempts to curb the illegal abuses by man.

The humorous side, the dangerous side and the tedious side all combine together to make one of the most interesting occupations in the outdoor field.

Even though most of the stories here took place years ago, recent cases investigated and prosecuted by the agencies prove there is still profit to be made deviating from the rules.

Outlaws on the Big River

Introduction.

Of the many things I inherited from my Dad, one of them was the gift of story telling. The other was the intense desire to one day become an Oregon State Police Game Warden or "State Bull" as they were referred to when I was growing up.

They are the Fish and Wildlife Officers of one of the most respected and admired State Police agencies in the country. It was a term of admiration by the outdoors crowd where I was raised. More than once I had occasion to be checked by the "Bulls", and every time I came away in awe of their command presence. We never knew when they would show up and that fact kept us from committing very many outdoor violations.

They would pop out of the woods or be waiting just around the next corner on the winding twisting remote gravel roads in the Cascade Foothills where I grew up and hunted. It always seemed that these highly trained but thinly spread wardens were able to be in several different places at the same time.

In 1962 I left home and joined the Air Force. 8 years and two Honorable Discharges later I returned to Oregon and was hired by the Oregon State Police. Some 3 years after that I secured a permanent position with the Fish and Wildlife Division of OSP.

My interests took me quickly to the Columbia River and the job of commercial fish enforcement. These stories are my recollection of actual events as they occurred. Over the years I had developed a keen memory for details and times. Although I occasionally get corrected by some of the other Wardens who were there, the facts will never change. At least not in my mind. Now 15 years after retirement we (wardens) get together at an annual camping event referred to as Cow Camp and swap tales. We all swear they are true. We all have our stories to tell.

I am now in my 15th year of retirement and still cannot totally divorce myself from enforcement. I serve on the Columbia River Recreational Advisory Committee and the Government Relations Committee with Coastal Conservation Association. Up until last spring I remained active in Law Enforcement with contract jobs in OSP and US Marshal Service.

I got my first chance at professional writing when one of my articles was published in a national magazine Tide, a publication of the Coastal Conservation Association.

I decided it was time to lay back, enjoy retirement and pursue my writing ambition.

Chapter I

Columbia River Pirates

Early in the spring of 1973 I was assigned to Commercial Fish Enforcement. The Wildlife Lieutenant asked me if I was a boat operator. I assured him I had operated all types of boats and I guess he believed me. In fact I had operated my own fishing and ski boats and had taken the wheel several times on my older brother's 28 foot cruiser. So I wasn't really faking it.

My fellow game officer, Bob and I decided it was time to go out and really explore the big river at night.

We had access to other trailerable boats that were adequate at best. Most of them were 16 foot Starcraft runabouts with a 55HP motor and canvas tops that usually leaked. We launched at one of the many ramps that put us close to the area we wanted to patrol. We had been out several times with the smaller boats confining our patrols to local areas and hugging the shorelines around Sauvie Island.

The 22 foot Seabird patrol boat was waiting for us in its slip at the Jantzen Marina. I checked off the starting procedures, fired it up and backed out into the dark, knowing some about what lay ahead. My course was set and I had an idea where I was going! And I had the feeling it was going to be interesting!

I won't go into the hair rising details of navigating the Columbia River at night with little experience but the near misses now seem like far off dim memories. Some of them are best forgotten.

Darkness provided cover and stealth but it also limited our visibility and safety. Fog was an added problem, at times so dense we were unable to see much beyond the bow of the boat. Watching the primitive depth finders kept us from running aground or straying into the deeper water where huge freighters plied their way upriver to the docks in Portland.

Once while feeling our way along in thick fog I looked up and saw a red light above us and off about 50-75 yards. It didn't take long to comprehend it was a freighter moving slowly toward us. We quickly maneuvered the boat to get into the safety of shallower water.

The early 70s was still the time of gill net "pirates" on the lower river. They usually had faster boats and used that to their advantage. More often than not when we came across an illegal gill net, we heard a motor fire up and race off into the darkness. Learning the river, navigation skills and the hundreds of sites used by illegal gill netters was a challenge!

I remember an outdoor writer at The Oregonian newspaper describing how outlaw fishermen kept him awake racing around on the Columbia all night when he would camp on his boat.

It wasn't quite that bad but it was not an unusual incidence either!

As we fine tuned our operation we learned to use our lights less and slowly drift along the shadows of the riverbank, using the lights of the shore to back light the bad guys. Each patrol improved our knowledge of the river and its twists and turns.

The lower river, as it is referred to, consists of the free flowing portion from Bonneville Dam to the Pacific Ocean. Other than channel dredging it has remained the same river, tidally effected to the extent that the current turns and runs back in far up from the Pacific Ocean on an incoming tide. During the day the river looks peaceful and welcoming. At night it is a dark hole described best as "black as the inside of a cow".

When the clouds cover the sky and shore lights disappear in the distance you feel as if you are suspended in space with no sense of motion till you glance over the side and see the froth coming off the bow wake as it cuts the glassy surface.

Below Clatskanie where the river meets the estuary, it becomes a huge area of twisting channels and islands. In the daytime it is tricky to navigate outside the main channel to the inexperienced. At night it is downright daunting and baffling. Run aground on a sand bar on an outgoing tide and you are going to be there for 6-8 hours at least. At times the tide can cause the river to fluctuate as much as 6 feet from low water to high water.

It is home to wildlife ranging from Deer and Elk to Bald Eagles, Osprey, all sorts of waterfowl, Seals, Sea Lions and of course hundreds of thousands of fish. Add to this mix several hundred thousand people who live on or near the river and seek its bounty whether it be for sport, food or profit. Profit was the one that generated the most potential for illegal activity.

Fish runs came into the river in succession beginning with Winter run Steelhead, followed by Spring Chinook, Summer run Steelhead along with Summer run Chinook, Fall run Chinook, Coho Salmon followed again by Winter Steelhead. There was seldom a month of inactivity on the river. On top of the Salmon runs the Sturgeon fishery provided activity on a year round basis.

NABBING THE SET NETTERS

One of the first fish cases I was involved in began with a phone call at about 10:00PM. A Senior Officer from Portland called me and advised dispatch had a report of a set net during the regular fall Salmon gill net season somewhere near Dodson just below Bonneville Dam. Our job was to find it and if possible arrest those accountable.

Set nets are unlawful to use even during an open season. They are simply a gill net tied to a fixed object so they cannot drift freely. The nets fish all night in one spot with little or no effort on the part of the operator.

Senior Trooper Russ met me at the Jantzen Marina where the patrol boat was moored. We loaded our gear and headed upriver a distance of 25 miles or so. We had a hard east wind blowing out of the gorge and hit rough water at Troutdale some ten miles up from the marina. Russ excused himself and crawled into the cabin bunk to grab some sleep, secure that I could get us there safely.

I had never been on this stretch of river at night but was rather familiar with river lights and navigation markers. Even so with limited visibility, I knew it would be a long night.

Near Rooster Rock the river channel is close to the Washington side. The area is called Cape Horn and the current there is strong. The wind was howling and solid green water was hitting the windshield as the bow of the boat raised on each wave and plunged into the next one. The only lights are channel marker lights. Other than that it is total darkness. On long range stretches of the Columbia it is difficult to tell if you are even making forward progress, especially with the wind blowing directly at you. Strong currents couple with strong winds to make it much worse.

Looking across the river at Cape Horn on the Washington side above Portland.

I strained to see the next marker light and kept on course with the compass. We did not have radar or Loran in those days. I figured our progress was about two knots at best and it became a long night. Finally at the upper end of Skamania Island near Multnomah Falls we came into calmer waters.

Daylight was just breaking ahead and Russ joined me on the deck. "Good job" he mumbled after figuring out where we were. I was starting to get my morning high with the sun peeking over the mountains in the gorge. My eyes, deprived of light all night now squinted in the morning sun. We began creeping along not wanting to tip the locals off and scanned the river ahead.

One gill net boat was working the opposite side of the river and apparently did not see us. We soon spotted our target, a net about 1000 feet long tied to a piling across from a recreation area called Coverts Landing.

Coverts Landing on the Oregon side of the Columbia
River just below Bonneville Dam.

A small skiff was tied to one end of the long net. We approached and found two young lads sleeping in the skiff.

Russ rousted them out of their sleep, "Wake up boys, we have work to do!"

The young lads shook themselves awake and I noticed the gill net boat approaching. It was their father who seemed rather unhappy to see us with his two sons in tow. He claimed no responsibility, which didn't surprise either of us. We asked him if he would pull the net which was noticeably heavy with fall Chinook. He declined saying it was our problem not his and left with his two boys after we issued them citations for Fishing Prohibited Method and No Commercial Fishing License. There was no lenience for juvenile offenders when it came to large scale commercial violations.

After putting 1000 feet of net and 2000 pounds of fish on board we motored over to Rooster Rock to offload. Our Fish and Game Lieutenant and several other local supervisors were on hand to see the haul we had made.

By the time we offloaded, we were 12 hours into our shift and had several more hours to go back, clean the boat and write reports. The Lieutenant offered to buy us breakfast on the expense account!

We were just clearing the dock as Russ muttered, "Gee thanks you're all heart!"

There was no such thing as overtime in those days. It was referred to as" love time". It was just expected that you finished the job you started regardless of how many hours it took.

Several months later the boys appeared in juvenile court with the family Attorney. He argued the case and demanded we produce the net and the weights that held it down.

The Judge replied, "Are you serious? I don't want any dirty old gill net in my court room. If the officers say there was a gill net that's good enough for me! And what's more I'm tired of hearing about illegal gill nets on our rivers! The sentence will be $500 apiece and 10 days suspended on condition they keep their records clean for a year."

POACHERS IN THE DARK

We spent countless nights on the river during the Salmon seasons and many of those nights yielded nothing. One pleasant night the following spring, Trooper Leryl Brown and I were creeping up the Oregon shore along Sauvie Island weaving in and out of the wing dikes. We nearly ran into a set net hanging off one near Marshall Beach.

Leryl was one of the first really river savvy Troopers I had the pleasure to work with. He was some years younger but had been stationed on the river since his hiring. He and I shared a wealth of experiences in the short time I had at St. Helens.

Wing dikes are rows of pilings that had been driven into the river at right angles to the current. Their purpose is to channel the current to the center of the river thus hindering bank erosion and keeping the channel clear. They also diverted runs of salmon out and around the dike ends making a set net very efficient at that location.

*Anglers on thee lower Columbia relax at their rods, waiting for a
Salmon to hit their lures. Wing dike is in the background.*

We checked the net to make sure it was a fresh set. We didn't
want to be wasting time waiting for the return of the outlaws.

We backed off to hide our 20 foot patrol boat in the shadows
on the beach downstream and waited. About 3:00 AM we heard
a motor boat approaching from upriver. They went directly
to the red navigation light on the end of the wing dike and
began pulling the net as we watched with a night vision scope.
I started up the patrol boat and as carefully as possible motored
toward the netters. They never saw us until we bumped up
against their boat and lit them up with 500,000 candlepower
spotlights.

Trooper Brown took their picture with a Polaroid and greeted
them with, "Top of the mornin' to you boys, State Police."

They were just a couple of opportunists from the
Washington side of the river. They had little to say about their

failed endeavor. We took their boat, gear, 17 Spring Chinook and left them on shore with $1500 tickets. We felt pretty good about the night's work!

A Portland Judge later fined them $250 apiece and returned their boat after they had pled guilty! He was a new Judge and unfamiliar with commercial fishing laws. He assumed all he had before him were a couple of anglers that had caught too many fish. We learned another lesson. If we had any cases that involved commercial fishing, we would have to be in court when they appeared for arraignment so we could describe the offenses to the prosecutor and Judge. The courts were not interested enough in wildlife cases to look into the specifics.

We were irritated that our well planned arrests went up in smoke! I contacted some friends in Northwest Steelheaders, an association dedicated to preserving Salmon and Steelhead runs. They took turns calling the Judge and giving him a piece of their minds!

A week or so later I received a call from our Major in Salem who let me know the Governor was not happy with the phone calls the Judge was getting. He advised me the Governor had told him it better stop or someone was going to lose their job! And he assured me it was not going to be his! We called off the dogs.

AM SURPRISE

One of the most appealing aspects of fish and Wildlife enforcement was the control over your own schedule. All of our officers worked a preplanned itinerary but when times demanded it could be changed at a moments notice with a simple call to the dispatch, "Hey I'm going to work. Sign me in."

Spring Chinook season was a busy time of the year and I was enjoying a good night of sleep when I woke up at about

2:30 AM. I had the strange feeling that something needed my attention. Not really sure of what it was, I pulled on my uniform, kissed my wife goodbye and headed down past Rainier to Mayger Road, just following my instincts.

There were two fish receiving stations located on the river at the end of the road. Usually when we drove the road the commercial fishermen knew we were coming. Many of them lived along the way and the telephone alert system would warn anyone conducting illegal activity. Not this night evidently!

I drove into the upper Mayger fish station which was alive with commotion. The fish station sits perched on pilings over the river and is connected to the land by a rickety one lane bridge. People on the dock stared like deer in the headlights and then began running for cover.

Old upper Mayger fish station, once the center of commercial fish activity on the lower river, now crumbling into decay.

11

I jumped out and ran onto the dock just as one of the workers tossed some oversize Sturgeon chunks into the river. 4 people escaped into the brush while I struggled to detain the manager and his assistant. The dock was littered with undersize and oversize sturgeon carcasses in various stages of butchering.

Sturgeon are valuable commercial fish that have always been protected by regulation of slot limits. The fish had to be at least 48 inches in length and no more than 72 inches. It was always unlawful to cut these fish into pieces prior to arrival at the wholesalers. Once cut it is nearly impossible to establish the size of these fish.

One gill net boat approached the dock from the river and as I looked down I could see an oversize Sturgeon in the stern of the boat. It was bent in a U shape from gunnel to gunnel. Judging the boat at 10' beam put the fish well over 10'. I told him to tie up and he replied "screw you" as he throttled off into the main river.

Shortly I saw a big splash as he returned the fish to the depths. I never saw him or his boat again. I guess he was not intimidated by my authority. By this time I was really wishing I had a partner with me. I was badly outnumbered but I had the element of surprise! I had really never been threatened by any of the commercial fishermen as most were hardworking family men.

Once I was able to secure the scene, over 3500 pounds of illegal Sturgeon was seized. At the time it was probably worth some $7000 on the black market. The manager and his helper insisted they had been set up! But they couldn't explain how that would have happened.

During the short trial the defense attorney kept asking why I just happened to show up at the right time. He insisted

I must have had a phone call and wanted me to tell him who had called to report the violation. Attorneys that were not well versed in defending commercial fish cases often tried to attack from different angles.

He had a hard time believing my story that I just "woke up out of a dead sleep and drove to the scene." I never did figure out what his angle was. Even if I had been called, I don't know how that would have changed anything. No one was forcing them to break the law.

I replied, "You will just have to believe it because it is the truth."

These were slam dunk cases because we usually caught them red handed. Finding them guilty was easy. Getting substantial fines and penalties was not.

The Astoria Judge found them guilty and gave them a whopping $250 fine apiece despite the objection of the District Attorney! It was getting mighty disappointing with those puny fines. It was just a cost of doing business to the outlaws and did not set much a deterrent. Our only alternative was to put enough pressure on them and force them to obey the rules.

HIDDEN NETS

Nearly every night during the Spring Chinook run we would drag the river around Mayger and Clatskanie with grappling hooks and find at least one diver gill net. These nets would be tied to a piling or dock, stretched into the current and weighted with heavy objects completely submerging them so that nothing on the surface could be seen.

Here nearly every night during the Spring Chinook runs, illegal nets could be found, hanging off the pilings and stretched out into the river.

We would hide the boat and wait until daylight to see if we could catch them pulling the nets. In the morning the illegal netters would turn their dogs out and more often than not find one of us hiding in the brush. Of course they always denied any knowledge of the nets or who set them.

One old timer started yelling at us while we were pulling an illegal net off the upper Mayger station. He was bold enough to accuse us of stealing nets! We asked him if he wanted to claim possession of this one and the citation that would go with it. He dazzled us with his colorful language and left us to our work.

A number of years later I became friends with a man who related a story of his near miss with me in the brush. He was teaching school at the time in Rainier and had accompanied one of the locals on a "fishing expedition". We had located their net and were searching the brush in the dark. He said I nearly stepped on him in the high grass before turning around. He was so frightened by the incident he never repeated it again. He said he could imagine the headlines. "Local School Teacher Arrested"!

During those years we put a huge amount of enforcement pressure on the river and places of business. Night after night we patrolled the river in random patterns trying our best to keep the scofflaws off guard. Many nights yielded nothing for our efforts. But every so often we would come into the right place at the right time! Surprise was often our best weapon!

PROCESSORS AND RESTAURANTS

Custom canneries were places where illegal fish could easily be funneled into the open market. They took in both sport and commercial caught fish, smoked and canned them. The sport caught fish were supposed to be kept separate and not sold or traded. They were only allowed to be processed for individual fishermen.

The commercial fish were bought and sold to the public under the wholesale retail laws. These businesses were often targeted and cited often for possession of gill net caught Steelhead and closed season Chinook or Sturgeon. Usually sloppy record keeping brought on by greed was their demise.

No commercial business that had the means to move fresh fish was beyond suspicion. High end hotels and restaurants in the Portland area were often found in possession of undocumented Spring Chinook. They could buy the fish much cheaper on the black market than on the legal open market.

Steady checking was essential because the fish would move through the businesses so fast. Regulations required any commercial enterprise to keep precise records of all fish they bought and from whom they bought it. But once the fish were disposed of there was nothing left to check.

One of our Drug Enforcement officers tipped us off to a local pimp in the Portland area who had an unusual side business going. It seemed one of his clients liked to pay with "product" as he called it. We located an old ice storage building he had rented and filled with illegal salmon, frozen whole. Fish frozen this way kept for almost a year with no deterioration. He told us whenever he needed easy money he used a band saw, cut a couple of boxes of salmon steaks, wrapped them in fancy tissue paper and sold them to local outlets for $10 - $15 a pound.

One custom cannery gave up the business after going to court many times and losing every case. They took one case to the Court of Appeals on the grounds we were harassing them with our constant random checks.

The Court of Appeals ruled in favor of the State with the presiding judge stating; "If you choose to enter a pervasively regulated business, you can only expect to be pervasively regulated".

I really liked that Judge!

Chapter II

Outlaws on the River

Dealing with fish poachers on the Columbia River in the 60s and 70s was a constant learning experience both for the thinly spread enforcement men and those who chose to operate outside the laws.

All that was needed to make pockets full of cash was a 14-16 foot boat with enough power to carry a load of fish, net and one or two poachers. Big boats, radar or night vision gear, were barely accessible to enforcement at the time.

It became a game, though a dangerous one, of cat and mouse, of who had the most nerve to race off down river in total dark in flight and pursuit. In addition to floating logs, navigation aids, some which were lighted, some which were not, wing dikes often covered by high water or high tides and ever changing sand bars, the lower Columbia River was a challenge at night to the inexperienced.

I recalled a class we had in basic training when I enlisted in the Air Force. They taught us how to increase our night vision. Over time we were able to see objects in the dark that were not visible to the untrained eye. Turning on the lights would dampen night vision.

Reporters and Supervisors who rode along occasionally were prone to grab the dash and inhale deeply when we ran at high speeds without lights. Knowing the river, where you were and keeping close lookout was necessary to stay out of harm's way.

Both Washington and Oregon patrol the Columbia under concurrent jurisdiction of the Columbia River Compact. Washington Department of Fisheries and Wildlife was and still is an Agency dedicated to Commercial Fish Management Enforcement and usually with superior equipment. Along the lower river there were Washington Agents at Vancouver, Longview, Skamokawa, and Ilwaco. Oregon had Officers at Portland, St. Helens and Astoria.

Oregon State Police operate as the primary Law Enforcement body charged with enforcement of all State laws. From its beginning in 1931 it was divided into Patrol, Criminal, Arson and Fish and Wildlife Divisions. After a gradual phasing out of a few Department of Fish and Wildlife Enforcement Agents, ODFW became the management agency and handed the enforcement over to Oregon State Police. Officers assigned to the Fish and Wildlife Division were further broken down into Wildlife and Commercial Fish Enforcement.

Training for river duty on the Oregon side consisted of getting hands on and doing the job most often with a senior officer who had experience in the field. There were a few specialized watercraft stationed on the coast but river patrol boats were often purchased through sport boat manufacturers with little thought to their enforcement use. Slowly the boats became more job and area specific and officers became more comfortable in their roles on the river.

While there were plenty of serious moments, the job fairly lent itself to amusing incidents. If anything could go wrong it would go wrong on the river at night. The first thing a rookie had to learn was that when ships pass by they tend to suck all the water out from beneath your boat if you are in shallow water.

We met up with a Portland patrol one night and were sitting in a little cove drinking coffee and talking. My partner saw the ship approaching and silently signaled to get into deeper water. We eased away from them and when the water left the cove their patrol boat keeled over at a 45 degree angle.

The operator was frantically trying to engage the prop in the mud. Just about then the water came rushing back in from the wake and shoved them further into the cove. We were rolling with laughter but they didn't see the humor of it all.

REELING THEM IN

Farther downriver where the tide flats stretched for hundreds of yards, two officers were creeping along in the fog and ran across a gill net floating in shallow water.

The lower tidal area of the Columbia River upstream from Astoria stretches for miles and contains a puzzle of channels and islands.

Their 26 foot radar equipped patrol boat made a comfortable and safe work platform. Henry, one of the most experienced river officers I ever met was at the helm. He knew from his long time on the river what was probably at the end of the net.

Visibility was less than twenty yards and the net moved as if someone was pulling it. They quietly tied their patrol boat to the end and sat back hardly able to contain themselves as the unsuspecting poachers reeled them in. Picture the shock when the outlaws realized what they had caught! Or what had caught them!

JUMPING SHIP

Usually when the instant of confrontation arrives, adrenalin starts pumping. It becomes very hard to keep from jumping into the fray too soon.

We had come upon a gill net tied to a wing dike on Sauvie Island and after watching it for some time were able to make out several people apparently dozing in sleeping bags on the beach. They were unaware to our presence probably because the visibility was hindered by low clouds and no moon or shore lights. We decided to sit back until they actually pulled the net and then move in on them and make the capture.

We had our Department pilot along that night and he was eager to catch a poacher! We tied to a wing dike several hundred feet downriver and waited, keeping them under observation with night vision telescopes. These were the early Vietnam era scopes and lacked the detail of the newer ones. Basically we could make out shapes and terrain.

Suddenly the figures on the beach started moving and it appeared they were pulling the net. We wanted to capture them in the act to reduce their chances of hightailing it into the woods nearby. We made a run at the beach with the intent of hitting the beach and jumping ashore. We didn't realize a small sand bar extended between us and the beach. Dave was poised on the bow of the boat ready to jump! 10 feet from the beach the boat hit the sand bar and launched him head first over the bow into the shallow water wounding only his pride. Our targets fled through the brush and escaped.

We did recover the net and fish and several sleeping bags. And we had a good idea who the poachers were. They would be the subjects of future arrests!

RICHARD AND MARVIN

A pair of serious poachers operated on the river between Portland and Astoria in the early 70s. Washington Fisheries had made arrests on these two before.

In one incident the Washington boat attempted to overtake the two during a closed season fishing incident. One of them pulled a rifle and pointed it at the patrol boat. Washington Agents responded by driving the pointed bow of their solid aluminum, patrol boat through the hull of the poacher's wooden boat sinking it in the shallow water. Aluminum trumps wood every time!

One of these outlaws owned a Columbia River gill net permit and operated when he wanted. To him the season was open when fish were present. Even during the open season he seemed ignorant to the laws governing the proper care and handling of Salmon.

We were summoned to North Portland one warm afternoon to investigate a U Haul van that had a strong stench of rotting fish. The truck had been abandoned on a side street and contained several hundred pounds of maggot infested salmon. A quick check with U Haul dealer identified the commercial fisherman as one of our regulars. We contacted him and issued citations for waste of food fish. His only defense was that he couldn't find a buyer for the fish and had to get some sleep! So he simply parked the van and left it.

One night in March of 1973 after the winter gill net season was over, two St. Helens Officers set up surveillance at Warrior Rock on the lower end of Sauvie Island. There is an abandoned lighthouse on the rock and the windows had been boarded up. One of the officers worked his way into the lighthouse and drilled a small hole in the plywood covering the window. He was able to see the entire area around the rock.

Before long the netters came and set their net in the eddy just below him. He was able to watch their actions, wait till they were in the middle of pulling the net full of fish and call in the troops. They were arrested, their boat, net and fish seized and were given a court date.

Several days later I was conducting a commercial fish check on one of the higher end restaurants in the area. Their product and records appeared to be in order so I left. When I got back to the office I got a call from an employee of the restaurant. He told me I had missed the illegal fish which were kept in a cold storage room several blocks from the restaurant. I went back to the manager and asked him about the storage facility, careful not to give any hint of who had turned him in.

The laws gave us the authority to check any business and its premises that dealt in fish or seafood for proper source records. He readily showed me the storage facility but could not produce records for some thirty fresh frozen Spring Chinook he had there.

I called ODFW to arrange an audit of their books. Upon examining the books the auditor located a $1500 check written to the same person who had been arrested at Warrior Rock. The check was written two days before his arrest and listed the sale of 300 pounds of fresh caught Spring Chinook; two weeks after the season had closed!

He was met in court several weeks later with his attorney to answer the other charges. We presented him with a new set of charges based on the sale of fish to the restaurant.

He responded whining, "It's just no fun anymore. It used to be like a game running from you guys on the river. Now you come up with stuff like this!"

As the equipment on the river improved, patrols were increased. Safety and comfort was no longer compromised. Patrols from Portland overlapped St. Helens and patrols from St. Helens overlapped Astoria. Commercial fish enforcement demanded a high priority.

RIVER CLOSURES

During the fall gill net season we were returning upriver from Astoria after working the gill net opener there. The river above Tongue Point was closed to gill netting and we were not anticipating much action. However we were operating in the dark mode with no lights and observing the river ahead on radar.

Astoria East End Mooring Basin looking upriver
toward Tongue Point.

As we passed under the bridge from Cathlamet to Puget Island we noticed a blip on the radar screen about 1 mile ahead. We slowed and used the night vision scope to scan the area. The water was mirror smooth and a string of floats stretched nearly across the channel. Off to one side and downstream was a bow picker, drifting, with its lights off. We naturally assumed they were the ones who had set the net.

We continued slowly upstream until we were within a few hundred yards, activated our lights and approached the boat. Two men were on the boat and acted rather surprised to see us. My partner boarded their boat and questioned them about the net. They denied any knowledge of it and insisted they were simply out for a ride on the river. The boat showed no signs of recently having a net on board. In fact it had cobwebs on the net roller and the deck was clean. We had no choice but to take their names and addresses and let them go.

The tide had begun to run out and the net began drifting toward the bridge. Before long it would be wrapped around the bridge piers. It was full of fall Chinook and we did not want to have to wrestle it off the piers. Pulling it quickly was our only choice. Fish, net and trash came into the boat in one huge mess.

We later determined there were 1200 pounds of fish plus one wet 1000 foot net. A phone call brought Astoria Troopers to the Westport boat ramp to meet us, offload the fish and we continued on our way home.

No case was ever made. Rumors later surfaced that a couple of locals were laying low after their near miss.

ONE NIGHT AT THE BAR

One night awaiting the Spring Chinook season opener we were moored at Warrenton Marina just downriver from Astoria. The season did not open till the next day and we were set to spend the night on the boat.

Dispatch called us and reported they had received reports of a gill net boat working the bar area near Buoy 10. On an outgoing tide this is one of the more dangerous parts of the Columbia River Bar, which is known as the Graveyard of the Pacific.

I had worked the bar many times in daylight during the sport seasons but never at night. We felt secure we could navigate it at night with radar and set out to see what we could find. We should have at least notified the Coast Guard we were going out. As we eased out of the harbor into the main river conditions looked calm. We were just out on another boat ride!

It was fairly easy to see the red and green buoy lights marking the channel but the further we proceeded down the river the rougher it got. By the time we were two miles from Buoy #10 where the river meets the ocean we were in 6-8 foot swells with a hard outgoing tide. We shot past one buoy so fast I thought for an instant it was another boat passing us in the opposite direction.

We quickly realized we were in over our heads and started looking for a way out. The swells were getting closer together and reversing direction had to be done quickly to avoid broaching. We did not want to end up on the treacherous Columbia River Bar in total darkness! We lit up the area ahead and saw a flat area of water, made our move and got the boat turned against the current. Now we had to boost the power to avoid the following seas.

It took us less than 15 minutes to get downriver to Buoy 10 and about an hour to get back upriver where we started. As we continued upriver the water and current conditions subsided. We finally reached the safety of the harbor and tied up again for the night. It amazed me how good the bunks felt and how easily sleep came on a boat after we were once again safe in our moorage.

We really didn't think much about the circumstances until later. We had come close to Clatsop Spit where shallow water turns the outgoing tide into a tangle of white caps and waves. Here it is possible to run aground in the trough of a swell and capsize when the next wave breaks over the stern. More than one small craft has met its end in that water.

No one could have possibly been netting in those extreme conditions. We concluded we had been set up with a phony call. Had anything happened, engine failure, broaching, no one would have even known where to start looking. Call us lucky! It was just part of the job. But better yet it was another lesson learned!

Mouth of the Clatskanie River where it enters the Columbia.

DEADLY CONFRONTATION

Another perilous situation arose upriver during a closure in the spring. Again we were drifting slowly downriver without lights at about midnight when we saw a commercial boat come out of the Clatskanie Channel about 300 yards off our port side.

Looking downriver from Astoria, Astoria Megler Bridge.

We shut down to observe and the boat continued out into the river toward us. When it appeared he was coming fast directly at us, I switched on our running lights. He continued on directly toward us and lit us up with his spotlight. I abruptly realized we had to get out of his way or be run down! We had a 21 foot boat and his was a much heavier 30 foot bow picker. It didn't matter which way I turned he kept coming at us as if he wanted to ram us!

Luckily our boat was more maneuverable but I could not outrun him. He had much more power and speed. After several near misses it became clear our lives were in danger and deadly force became a decision. This is not something any police officer wants to do but we had no choice. I situated the boat so I could take advantage of the starboard side cabin window and Trooper Brown got out on the deck. Both of us had weapons drawn and pointed at the boat operator when he decided to end it and shut his engine down.

We both knew the operator and by all indications he had been drinking. He was still in a confrontational mood and rather than getting into an ugly conflict in the middle of the river in March we ordered him to go home and meet with us in the morning. His passenger agreed to take the controls.

Law enforcement on the river often required inventiveness. On land we would have arrested the man and taken him to jail. On the water, at night, in cold weather conditions too many things can happen. We knew most of the fishermen and where they lived. Risking lives over violations that were treated lightly by the courts just did not add up.

The next day we met him at his home and discussed the circumstances of the night before. He had no explanation for his actions other than he just got upset at seeing us out there. He apologized and admitted he had too much to drink. He was issued a number of citations for Reckless Boat Operation, Assault and Reckless Endangering.

Unfortunately the local DA disagreed with the charges and dismissed them on a technicality. He agreed we would have had reason to use deadly force but would not prosecute on the charges. As things turned out, we were both relieved we did not have to use deadly force.

I don't know if, to this day, the fisherman realizes how close he came to ending his career and his life.

It was always a good thing to end a day going home safely to our families.

Chapter III

No one ever said work had to be boring.

And it certainly wasn't working the Columbia River as a Commercial Fish Enforcement Officer with OSP. A good bit of police work consists of talking to people and listening to what they are saying and how they are saying it. Their body language can tell you what you want to know without them even being aware they are doing it.

Law enforcement officers over the years develop what is called the "thousand yard stare". They are always surveying the area around them and people often think they aren't listening because their eyes continually wander looking for that something that just isn't right. It's not rudeness, it's just being aware of your surroundings and it is very difficult to turn off.

With experience you can just about guess what a person is going to say as they walk up to you, even if they are total strangers. Most crooks including serious game violators get caught because they just cannot resist the attraction to talk about their deeds. One of the most telling moments in an investigation interview was the moment the conversation turned and went something like this.

"Let's say someone did what you are accusing me of. What would the penalties be?"

At that point you knew the confession was about to come forth.

I DARE YOU...

Often when out at a restaurant we would see someone approaching and try to guess what they were going to say before they got there. More often than not we were right. One instance, four of us were having late dinner at a local cafe.

Three wranglers were sitting at a table across from us with their heads together obviously enjoying what they were planning to do. They would look at us, put their heads together and finally one of them got up looking brave and started for our table looking at me.

"They are settling a bet," I said. "I'll handle this."

The young cowboy started to speak, "Hey my buddies over there—"

I interrupted, "Let me finish this for you. They offered you some money to come over here and punch one of us in the mouth, right? How much?"

"Twenty bucks," the cowpoke replied sheepishly. "How did you know?"

I said, "Oh I don't know. Just a lucky guess! Tell you what pardner, you can throw your punch, get your ass kicked for twenty dollars and go to jail or you can sit down here real nice and have a beer! Which will it be?"

He walked back to the table and said something to his buddies and they quietly left. We got a good laugh out of that one.

LAMEST EXCUSES.

Part of our job was checking fish processors, restaurants and seafood dealers for legal product. Whether some of these business operators were naive, dumb or thought they could cover their tracks with lies, they never ceased to amaze us with their dumb stories.

The head chef of a high end Portland hotel and restaurant chain was contacted on a routine commercial fish inspection of the restaurant kitchen. A half a dozen Spring Chinook were in stock and fresh fish were on the menu.

He was unable to produce records for the fish and off the top of his head said he "bought them from a Polish trawler."

He became more puzzled when I asked him how they were delivered. I already had a good idea where the fish had come from. Polish trawlers did not operate in our waters and they didn't deliver salmon! I was enjoying the story he was so desperately trying to put together! He shrugged and accepted the citation and the receipt for the seized fish.

The trial went with no trouble and resulted in an easy conviction. The fine, as I recall, was heavy but the anger of the hotel manager was even heavier!

He berated the poor chef in the hall outside the courtroom for making everyone look stupid." Polish trawler indeed! What were you thinking?"

In addition to the fine Oregon Liquor Control Commission suspended their liquor license for 30 days!

CHANGES IN THE NIGHT!

I was conducting an early morning check of a local fish market and while there I noticed a couple of bright Steelhead in the display case advertised as Salmon.

Steelhead had just been made a game fish by initiative petition and it was illegal to sell or buy them.

I didn't want them to know I had spotted the Steelhead so I just I asked them where they bought their fish. They replied they had been delivered by a major fish wholesale distributor on the east side of Portland.

I called the officer that worked that area and he made a quick check of their location finding more Steelhead. The manager there insisted he had delivered nothing but Salmon to the market and had left them on the rear entrance in an iced container. The market operators steadfastly denied consciously receiving the Steelhead. Both the wholesalers and retailers were cited into court.

In court the defense attorney raised the possibility that someone had come along and switched the Salmon for Steelhead before they had been taken inside.

In his remarks while finding them guilty the judge made humorous reference to the absurd notion of a "mysterious night rider" going from business to business switching fish! Even the Judges had a sense of humor!

DON'T SAY YOU WEREN'T WARNED

One wholesale/custom canner on the mid Columbia had been cited many times for record violations and illegal fish. When I was promoted and assigned to The Dalles, I wanted to pay him one last visit just to say good bye. He really was quite a nice guy in spite of all his transgressions. We talked a while and then he told us he was receiving some fish later that morning from upriver. He even told us they were tribal ceremonial fish. I commented that he had better not receive those fish as they were illegal to have on commercial premises.

We left and drove down the road to wait. Sure enough, an hour later a vehicle turned into his place and two fishermen got out. We waited a few minutes, drove back and found them unloading several dozen fish. We told them they had been warned and they produced an altered permit that had the storage location crossed out and changed.

We had made the call beforehand to The Dalles to confirm that the location change had not been authorized at that end. The fish were seized, the operator cited and convicted in court, – again! They couldn't say they weren't warned!

LANGUAGE BARRIERS

Communication skills were extremely important when getting the job done. I went into a Japanese sashimi bar one day and talked to the manger. I told him I wanted to do a fisheries check and he invited me in to the kitchen. Right away I spotted two Steelhead soaking in water on the counter.

"Why do you have Steelhead here?' I asked. My mind was on the illegality of the fish.

"Sashimi" replied the chef.

Again I asked, "yes but why Steelhead?"

"They taste better", replied the chef.

Realizing we were on different wave lengths, I changed tactics. "Steelhead is illegal to serve in Oregon."

"Ah!" he replied as the meaning sunk in.

COLD HARD FACTS

One day early in the spring around 1976 we received a call from a marina operator at Goble, Oregon, between St. Helens and Rainier. He told us there had been suspicious activity after dark for several nights and he saw a couple of guys he didn't recognize loading out a boat early in the morning. We told him not to contact them if he saw them again. We set out in the patrol boat from St. Helens the following night after dark.

After some searching we located a net tied to the Washington shore just above the mouth of the Kalama River. We called our local USFW Service Agent and asked him to come out and cover the boat ramp while we waited in the boat upriver from the net.

It was extremely cold that night and we had our kerosene heater going in the cabin. We tied up to one of the industrial docks at Kalama and waited.

An hour or so later a security guard came down the dock and was checking things out. The dock level was probably 12-14 feet above our boat and he stood there and smoked a cigarette for 5-10 minutes. We did not want to alert him and have him light us up so we just hunkered down and hoped he wouldn't notice. He finally left and we went back to waiting.

Dave called about 0300 and advised there was a boat with two persons leaving the dock and heading across the river.

We carefully fired up and followed them back to the dock where the arrests were made without incident.

Their lawyer pleaded with the Judge "Your honor, the boat isn't paid for yet. My clients are still making payments on it."

The Judge replied, "Then I guess they will be making payments on nothing.

Chapter IV

The Tribal Fishery

Seven years into my career an opening for promotion to Corporal arose in The Dalles, Oregon, the center of the Tribal Fishery. I had been aware of the action those officers encountered on a weekly if not daily basis. Things were quite busy there! Tribal fishermen were challenging State authority and conflicts were frequent. It looked like a very interesting place to be as things were getting dull on the lower river.

I applied for the job and got it, then wondered if I had really thought this one out. It meant uprooting the family, putting the kids in a new school system and giving up a nice home we had built in the country. But The Dalles turned out to be a pleasant place to live and raise children.

I dove into the job right away and set out to see what all this new area was about.

The Columbia River above Bonneville Dam is referred to, of course, as the "Upper River". It is a series of impoundments behind monstrous hydroelectric dams built to provide power, navigation and flood control to the Northwest. The river banks were carved out of mostly solid basalt by a series of huge floods at the end of the ice age.

The beauty and archeological history of the area is incredible! Native Americans have been living there for thousands of years, gathering fish and game from the rich area surrounding the river. Lewis and Clark visited the area on their journey to the sea and reported on the bounty in their journals.

I had memories of the area prior to the construction of The Dalles and John Day Dams in the 1950s and how my Dad would stop and buy fish from the people along the river. I knew I was going to enjoy this assignment!

The Dalles Dam. Tribal fishing platforms hang from the rocks.

PLEASED TO MEET YOU!

Two other officers and I were checking fishermen near the John Day Dam on a nice afternoon when we ran head on into two of the toughest tribal fishermen around. At least according to the officers who knew them. I figured it was a good time to meet them so we proceeded with the fish check.

Now I can't even remember what the violation was. It was relatively minor but one of the fisherman was determined he was going to let me know who he was. A shouting match ensued and before it could turn really ugly he spit on my shoes!

"That's it! You're going to jail!" I shouted.

Handcuffs were applied and then one of the older Wardens pulled me aside. "Geez Corporal, we don't usually jail them for minor offenses! How about we settle down and rethink this?"Cooler heads prevailed and a citation was issued and they went on their way.

The other Warden remarked, "Well you made an impression on him! I'll bet he doesn't spit on your shoes anymore. "

It was funny! It became the buffer to several other confrontations.

JUMP!

One of the Officers, who worked there, had played college and pro football. He was in excellent physical condition and in addition was a self taught student of Native American Culture, an asset that was valuable during a later incident. He understood the culture and the people! He became locally famous for his ability to sit on the rocks near the end of the nets that were tied off to shore and wait quietly in the dark until the fishermen came close to untie the net. He would then jump into the boat and talk the fishermen into surrendering even though they sometimes outnumbered him 3 to 1.

While not in the training manual of police practices, it became very effective. One night one of the other officers decided to try it and mistimed the jump! He ended up in the water but kept a death grip on the boat. He was eventually successful in the capture though somewhat uncomfortable to relate the true facts of the case.

Every week during the salmon runs there were incidents and arrests on both sides of the river. Enforcement authority extended bank to bank for both Oregon and Washington.

LINES OF JURISDICTION

One night a boat chase on the river ended up with the fishermen beaching their boat on the Washington shore and heading off into the brush. Pursuit brings the adrenaline levels up and the Officers continued the foot chase up to the highway and detained the violators.

Our Department Major in Salem was not in a good mood when he heard the details. After he finished chewing me on the phone he calmed down a bit and asked what it would take to keep our officers from exceeding their jurisdiction. We decided a bow rope length distance from the boat would be the limits of their authority. Of course we lengthened the bow rope slightly!

Joint patrols with Washington and the U.S. Fish and Wildlife Service solved most of the land jurisdictional problems after that.

SHOTS FIRED!

On one of these joint patrols we chose to use some different tactics. One boat would leave Cascade Locks, head upriver and an hour later another one would follow. We knew from practice that the fishermen waited for the boat patrols to go by then began their illegal operations. The U.S. Fish and Wildlife boat left and an hour later we launched behind them.

We had just gone underway when a call for assistance came over the radio. They were taking small arms fire from an encampment on the Washington side of the river! Our boat was capable of 50+MPH and the distance was quickly covered.

We arrived on scene expecting to find some kind of activity but everything appeared to be quiet. There was no wind and the surface of the river was mirror smooth. Visibility was good considering the lack of lights on the shoreline. The night was eerily quiet and the only sound was the humming engine below the deck of the patrol boat. Things got rather tense when we realized the other boat was not in the area. We didn't know where they were. I throttled down and was cruising about 50 yards offshore of the encampment when a blast of pressure went by my nose instantaneously followed by the sound of the gunshot! There is no doubt left in your mind when you hear the sound of gun fire and realize it was directed at you! It was one of the more terrifying moments of my entire career! We looked at each other reassured to see no one had been hit!

I turned the boat away as another round hit the water directly in front of us. Several more shots were fired! We could not tell where the shots were coming from and returning fire was out of the question. We knew there were too many people and possibly children camped at that location. Our only alternative was to get the hell out of there!

I quickly turned to boat away from the line of fire and slammed the throttle forward. We were sitting ducks for whoever was shooting at us from the shoreline! We raced across the river toward a protective cove of rocks and located the other boat there that had taken fire. Great minds think alike!

We called in the ground forces of local Deputies from Washington and waited while they secured the scene. We then motored back across the river and into the small boat basin that served the landing.

Police were all over the place and in the back of my head I kept thinking about the bow rope warning we had received from headquarters. We were in the State of Washington!

We went ashore and gave our accounts to the local Deputies. They arrested the wife of the leader of the site. She told the Deputies she was only trying to scare us. She had no intent of hitting us!

Cook Landing Tribal in lieu site for Tribal fishermen and the scene of many conflicts over Tribal fishing rights as well as the scene of the shooting that occurred one night as patrol boats passed by offshore.

I sarcastically thanked her for her consideration and her careful aim. Later I played the scene over in my head and counted my blessings. A 50 -75 yard shot in the dark at a moving boat and missing my face by inches with a 30-06! Life was good! I often think about that shot in the dark and the possibilities of an imperfect aim, in the dark, at a moving object?

We ended the patrol for the night, exchanged notes, and congratulated each other for being alive and able to go home. All I wanted to do was get some sleep and forget about the night before.

KEEP THE BRASS INFORMED!

I was rudely awakened by the Sergeant in charge of the office later that morning when Headquarters called demanding a report of the incident. It had made the morning news outlets and Administrators didn't like to be uninformed! While disturbing to us, it had become just another in a long string of incidents we encountered on the river.

I calmly assured the powers to be that we were all safe and secure and things had been handled well. In the future, I promised that I would carefully keep them advised of any and all incidents.

Today the OSP Fish and Game Monthly reports are some of the most popular reading on local internet outdoor sites. The tiniest of incidents are covered in detail and serve as a deterrent to those who may be inclined to break wildlife law as well as a report to the public on how well their enforcement dollars are being spent. And the Administrators are kept informed!

ACTING NORMAL!

Every so often the Administrative Supervisors would come out and work on the river with us. Most of them had been in the field at one time or another and there were some light moments to share. One night the Lieutenant and Captain were along in the boat and we were searching the shore for nets.

We found one just about the time the boat engine decided to quit for the night. It was not a problem as there was another boat our upriver from us so we radioed our position and told them to come get us at daylight.

We anchored and watched the net figuring the fishermen would see us and leave. There was nothing else we could do. Now remember, we are in a 24 foot blue patrol boat well known to all the fishermen, anchored in open water alongside a small island less than 100 yards from the illegal net!

It was just turning daylight when we spotted the fishermen coming for their net. We had to sit there and watch them powerless to do a thing.

The Lieutenant was excited and hissed" Cover your badge!"

I looked and he was crouched over in the boat, in full blue uniform with his hand over his badge! As if it would cover up our identity! The humor of the situation struck me and I started laughing. The Captain was laughing also and the Lieutenant at first failed to see the humor.

There were times you just had to say, "What the hell?"

The two fishermen had odd looks on their faces when they went by in their boat, unable to quite appreciate why three game wardens were laughing at them and making no attempt to catch them.

For a long time after that when we would be in a situation someone would crack, "cover your badge!" It always got a laugh.

The local crew at The Dalles and the two outposts of Hood River and Arlington had a total of seven Troopers assigned Fish and Wildlife duties. They were the most experienced bunch of troops anyone could bring together. Walt and Mike worked out of Arlington, a small town just above the John Day Dam. Both had years of experience on the river and worked together very well. The practical jokes they played on unsuspecting Troopers are legend to this day. One night while conducting surveillance near the grain elevators on the river they called a Patrol Officer by radio to bring them some sandwiches.

They convinced the Trooper they were on the top of the grain elevators and could only be reached by climbing the ladder on the outside of the elevator! In fact they had their rig hidden where they could watch the perplexed Trooper trying to decide whether he really wanted to help out his fellow Troopers. When he finally decided to begin the ascent they relented and told him where they really were!

Roger, a former Marine, one who could be counted on to be the most level headed and Fred, one of the craftiest investigators I had ever run across held down the Hood River area.

The Dalles team consisted of Joe who worked even when he didn't have to, Fred, a dogged, thoughtful warden who always got his quarry and Bob, the youngest, toughest and the one we referred to as "jumper".

Just to add some variety to the job, we covered the lower section of the Deschutes River from North Junction to the mouth. The Deschutes is a popular Steelhead and Rainbow Trout fishery and is tightly restricted by State Parks. It is also a very trendy white water rafting area. We had two highly trained and qualified Cadets who worked the river in the summer out of The Dalles.

UP THE CREEK WITHOUT A PADDLE!

One day for a change of pace I accompanied them on a white water raft patrol. Now I have never claimed to be much of a swimmer and when the job required water duty I wore my life jacket.

I also brought my prized Canon 35 MM telephoto camera to get some action shots of the river. It was running pretty good early in April and the water temperature was hovering around 45 degrees.

We had just launched the raft below Sherars Bridge and I asked if I could take the oars. I settled into the rowing seat and instructed the Cadets to guard my camera at all cost.

One of the Cadets was humming the theme from the movie "Deliverance" as we shot through one mild set of rapids. A large spinning suck hole was coming up below and I set up the raft to slide by with the bow just over the hole. I miscalculated and when I realized it was too late I felt the raft pitch high. I knew we were going over and there was nothing to do but hang on!

The bow of the raft dropped and the rear shot up in the air and pitched me over the back! I vividly recall going straight to the bottom of the angriest piece of water I had ever been in. I was fully aware of my dilemma and was fighting to surface. The water was a mass of foam and bubbles and offered no flotation.

I thought to myself, "This is stupid! I'm going to die like this?"

Just then solid water grabbed my life jacket and I shot for the surface, gasping for dry air! I expected to see the raft upside down but there it was. Still upright with the two Cadets looking around to see where the Sergeant was.

Now I was cold, exhausted and heading downstream for another set of rapids. From training I knew not to try swimming against the current so I'm swimming downstream for the shore and the Cadets are trying to catch up with me in the raft. Thank God for the life jacket!

They finally got a line to me and reeled me in. I hooked one arm thru the rope on the side of the raft hung on, wanting no part of the cold water! When they finally pulled me onto the raft I just stretched out and enjoyed the moment. They wanted to take me back but I felt so good we finished out the drift drying my clothes in the warm sun.

I made them promise not to tell anyone about my event and they swore to it. Till we got to the office! Every wildlife officer I ever worked with hit the water once in his career. It's always a good story at the campfire gatherings. Mark, one of the Cadets is now a veteran Wildlife Officer still working in the same area. He enjoys telling the story I enjoy hearing him tell it! Thank you Mark!

DON'T HIT SOLID OBJECTS

In addition to the Oregon team we worked often with Washington Fish and Game Officers, Al, Dave and Paul, all experienced river professionals.

One night we conducted a joint patrol with Washington. Bob and Dave launched the boat in Hood River and Paul and I took the trailer to The Dalles where we agreed to meet at daylight. Paul and I worked along the shore on both sides.

The river here is bordered by I84 on the south and State Hwy 14 on the north. We spent the night watching the usual haunts and saw nothing.

By morning Paul and I started looking for the boat. We had heard nothing from them for several hours. We could not get any answer on the radio so we set out scanning the river. We were just above Klickitat, Washington when we heard a faint signal and voice calling for assistance.

We sped down the State highway watching for anything that might tell us where they were. As we passed a swampy area of cattails between the railroad tracks and the river I spotted what looked like a whip radio antenna poking up out of the cattails. Paul said he knew the road in there and we bounced across the railroad tracks and followed a trail to the river. There were Dave and Bob sitting on the bow of the patrol boat. The stern was almost underwater and both bilge pumps were spewing water out the sides. They were wet and grinning ear to ear!

Dave told us they were running upriver at high speed when they hit something hard. At first they thought they went over the top of a log but the steering became very difficult. The boat began to wallow and water started pouring over the floorboards.

Dave knew he had to get it out of deep water before it sank. With everything he could muster he turned the boat to shore and gave it all the throttle he had. The boat ran aground just as the engine flooded and quit.

Later it was discovered a large old timber that had floated off from and old dock in The Dalles was drifting just under the surface. It had put a hole almost 12 inches square just below the water line and turned the patrol boat into a submarine. Just another night on the water!

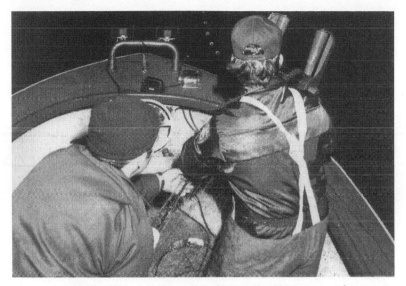

Two Oregon State Troopers pulling illegal nets at night.

USFWS Agents began playing big roles on the upper river also. 5 Special Agents, Dave, Ed, Elliot, Dick and many others lent expert support to the ongoing problems and gave us the flexibility we needed to move from one state to the other.

This group of dedicated Wardens and Agents went on to pull of one of the most successful and far reaching commercial fish cases ever prosecuted in the Northwest. Salmon Scam.

Chapter V

Tough guys!

I read once that over the entire country, assaults on police officers occur more frequently in Wildlife Enforcement than any other branch of Law Enforcement. I began mentally ticking off the string of incidents that occurred in the short several years I had been assigned to supervise the Tribal Fishery area. Minor assaults occurred often frequently ignored and not even acted upon.

I stand 6"6" tall and weighed in at 275 in my shorts while I was employed. I was always active, played sports and could take care of myself. Size usually discouraged the perpetrators from duking it out with the law! But that was no always the case.

It seemed the little tough guys often wanted to try out the big guy and I became very proficient at talking my way out of a fight. After all, they didn't pay us to fight, they paid us to keep the peace! Right?

Most of the Tribal fishermen were good natured people and we operated on a first name basis with many of them. But it was a constant battle trying to convince them to stick to the regulations.

TAKE ME TO JAIL!

I had just gone to bed one night and the phone rang.

A tribal fisher woman named Shirley was on the line and politely said, "Joe I want you to come down to Crates Point and arrest me. I'm fishing my dip net and I want you to arrest me."

This happened quite often as the Tribal people felt if they could get a case into court they would win, which ultimately happened. That's another story.

Any way I said "Shirley, I'm not coming down, go home and leave me alone."

She replied, "You have to come and arrest me. I'm breaking the law!" I could tell she was not about to go away quietly.

I put on my uniform, told my wife I would be back soon and left for the river less than a mile from my home. It was about 11:00PM and the area was unlit. I spotted a flashlight waving in the darkness by the river. I knew where the platform was that she and her boys fished.

Shirley was standing there with her dip net and one Steelhead and her noticeably intoxicated 18 year old son was standing beside her. I told her again to go home but she refused. I told her I would not take her to jail but would issue a citation instead. She agreed.

Tribal fishing platform. The long handled dip nets are lowered into the water to intercept Salmon swimming upstream. An ancient practice still in use today.

As I was writing the citation her son walked over next to me and tried to grab my book. Looking him in the eye, I told him firmly to stay away from me while I was writing. He ignored me and pulled again at my book. I shoved him aside and suddenly he came at me full speed. I grabbed his right arm and stepped under to put him into an arm bar takedown. He slipped out of my grasp and went flying to a rock wall headfirst.

At first I thought he had been knocked out cold or worse. The last thing I needed was a night of report writing.

As he dazedly got to his feet his mother pounced on him with her fists, screaming at him. "I raised you better than that!

How many times have I told you never to fight with a police officer?"

Now the poor kid was getting hammered and I had to hold back his mother from an assault on her son!

I finally got them calmed down enough to explain the citation and get them back to their car, exchanged small talk and headed home for the night.

YOU'RE THE COP, YOU FIND OUT!

A rather brutal beating occurred one night at Coberg Beach near Hood River. We were summoned to the scene by a couple of Yakima Tribal elders. Several of their younger fishermen had been beaten badly and threatened with guns. We searched the scene and found one loaded 9MM Auto handgun that had been lost in the sand. Blood splatters were all over the area. One of the elders, an old, weathered, but proud man insisted that we do our job and arrest the persons responsible. The victims knew who their assailants were but refused to tell us.

There was a code of sorts that prohibited them from identifying or causing the arrest of other tribal members by the "white cops". They simply refused to identify them and told us it was our job to identify and arrest them.

We were extremely annoyed at their lack of assistance and the case was never solved. They refused to believe we were there to help them.

The local wardens had become used to operating in a set method. When we discussed patrol tactics it became evident to me they had different methods than those I was used to on the Lower River. They did not believe in boat patrols and were convinced the locals watched the boat ramps, knew when the boats went out and where they were on the river.

The equipment in The Dalles was high quality. We had a 24 foot bow picker boat that had been custom built and was very fast and safe. It could handle hundreds of pounds of nets and fish and a crew of three.

I convinced the Troopers to use the boat and try some of the hide and wait tactics we had used productively. Some nights it worked too well!

Two OSP Troopers on patrol in the custom built bowpicker.

PREACHERS EDDY

Bob and I went up to Preachers Eddy, an old navigation light just below John Day Dam and a favorite netting spot of a group from Nez Perce Tribe. We located a net tied to the rocks and put together a plan. We had a rather old but stout Woolridge jet boat and we decided to tie right to the net and wait. The lighting from the Dam obscured us to anyone coming upriver.

Preachers Eddy light and Tribal platforms. The scene of many confrontations between Officers and Tribal fishermen.

It was a pleasant, warm night and we sat and talked about what we were going to do when they came to retrieve the net. The sound of a boat motor in the distance alerted us! A boat with several tribal fishermen approached the area slowly and was nearly within spitting distance when they saw us!

No pun intended but it was the same guy who had spit on my shoes! They raced off downriver in a boat that had twice the horsepower! We knew it was useless to chase. We pulled the net and the fish and headed for the boat ramp.

We were in the process of loading the boat and un-tangling the fish from the net when we were unexpectedly surrounded by about 7-8 young toughs looking for a fight! We were both on edge and not knowing what was coming next. It was useless to call for backup as at that time in the morning there was none to be had. They proceeded to circle us and taunt us with threats. Bob was a savvy confident man and persuaded me to ignore their threats.

They continued circling us and would reach out and tap us on the back while we loaded the gear and fish. It was as if they were counting coup. We finished our business and climbed into the cab of the truck. We poured some coffee and with the doors locked, windows rolled up, we sat there and enjoyed the scene playing out.

The men were infuriated by this time, drunk and begging for a fight but there was little they could do. I told Bob how close I came to striking out or even pulling a weapon. He agreed it was a close encounter but he knew the guys and how far they would go. I didn't. We made notes of who was there and what they had done for future reference.

CONVERSION

About a week later we met USFWS and Washington Fisheries at the Hood River boat ramp. The season was open for commercial fishing and while we stood there talking, a boat pulled into the marina.

I noticed the two were brothers and part of the group we had contact with at Preachers Eddy. One of them was the one who had spit on me.

The odds were now in our favor and I left the group, approached the two on the dock and requested we take a walk. I asked them if they had anything they wanted to say to us now that there were seven of us and two of them. I explained to them in no uncertain terms that if they really wanted a confrontation on the river we would not back down from them.

I assured them if there was to be a confrontation it would be one on one however. I was not going to be a referee. I wanted them to realize that when we were doing our jobs we did not expect a bunch of verbal or physical abuse from intoxicated people.

Both of the men apologized and assured me it would never happen again. I reminded them that we had been very fair about enforcement and never took anyone to jail unless they were unruly. That I also told them could quickly change.

I was not going to allow any of my Troopers to be assaulted or worse for doing their jobs. We shook hands, gave them citations to appear in court for the previous encounter and went home. I felt pretty good about the little "coming to an understanding" moment.

LESSONS LEARNED!

About a week after that we were again back up at Preachers Eddy. Bob had located another net tied off in the same closed area.

We had the big boat and decided to hide it in a lagoon behind the gravel piles downriver and wait. Bob would sit on the shore by the net and radio instructions. We also had a good idea who we were going to meet that night.

Washington Fisheries was in the river below with their patrol boat. A Trooper from the Fossil outpost was with me in our boat. He had never been on the river before and was looking forward to some action. He was about to get it!

Several hours went by then we heard a boat approaching from downriver. Bob radioed that they came to the net and pulled it and were coming toward us. I knew this time they could not outrun us. We waited and intercepted them as they went by.

I gunned the big bow picker up to speed and the chase was on. We easily stayed with them but they refused to stop. I had the powerful spotlights trained on their boat and the electronic siren yelping in the night. It must have been quite a sight from shore!

Dave came on the radio and said he was heading toward us and could see us coming at him. He made a perfect U turn as we went by and fell in alongside the outlaw boat. We had them boxed in with nowhere to go.

Solid basalt cliffs lined the shore to their right and two 5,000 pound patrol boats were herding them! Suddenly they swerved into the side of Dave's boat!

Dave called over the radio, "He hit me!" Next thing I see, the boat again tries to slam the side of Dave's boat.

Remember our speed was between 35-45 MPH, fast enough on the water! This time Dave was waiting and cut into the smaller boat. A huge wave erupted as the two boats collided and it looked like the smaller boat had been pushed under. Phil was awestruck and told me later he thought the fishermen were going to die! Dave shut down and his boat settled back in the water just as I pulled up to the disabled boat.

Here was two of the sorriest looking, wet to the bone fishermen standing defiantly in their boat half full of water with the outboard hanging by its cables. They were screaming at us with their fists clenched ready to fight.

I stepped on the bow of our boat and looked down at the two. "Hey guys, what about that talk we had?" It was the same two guys again.

They looked at me, instantly calmed down and said, "Sgt. Schwab could we have a ride back to get our truck, please?"

That was the last event we had with those two. On the way back to the ramp one of them was standing at the wheel with me like nothing had happened commenting about what nice boats we had and how fast they were. I knew deep down these were good people. Get their attention and respect and treat them with respect and most of the problems went away.

ROUTINE PATROLS

We were patrolling near Cook Inlet, a little in lieu site on the Washington side of the river, the same place the shots were fired. This is the area just above Wind Mountain. The river here is wide with few shallow spots.

We were coming upriver and spotted the wake of a smaller boat approaching above us. They could not see us and we were sure they were from the site heading home. We waited till they were within 50 yards and lit them up with the high powered spotlights.

They ran! The chase was on and we quickly closed the remaining distance between the two boats. I was at the wheel and Bob was ready to jump! At the speed we were traveling it was decided that was not a good option. The patrol boat had a steering station right on the open bow and I was able to look straight down and into their boat. We were cutting across the river at probably close to 45 MPH less than 3 feet apart! One misfire of their engine and we would be in their lap! I backed off slightly and gave them chance to stop. They finally decided they couldn't outrun us and their only option was to give up.

They had 20-25 illegal fish on board. We let them keep the boat as it wasn't worth our time to deal with it. The courts were giving them back anyway. It was just another routine night on the Bonneville Pool!

Not more than a couple weeks later we again found a setnet in the same area tied off to a navigation marker. Roger and I were in the boat and waited till the outlaws came for the net. We let them load it up and went to intercept them. The headed off toward the White Salmon River mouth at high speed. We simply followed in the wake 40-50 feet behind again with siren and lights on! As we passed under the Highway 14 bridge there were several sport fishermen on the rocks fishing for Steelhead. Here come two high speed boats splitting the water between them and into the White Salmon! The fleeing suspects never even slowed as they approached the shoreline. They hit the shore running the boat up high and dry and both leaped out in perfect fashion leaving the boat and gear behind as they fled into the night! We called Dave out and stood by until he could get there and take the boat, fish and gear into custody. The owners would be easy to find!

Scarcely a night went by that we didn't come upon someone trying to pull more illegal fish from the river. I can't recall how many outlaw boats were wrecked either by running them ashore at high speed or hitting solid rocks in the river.

RESCUE!

One afternoon I was at my desk in The Dalles finishing up some paperwork when a call came in that a Tugboat had capsized above Arlington near Threemile Canyon. I grabbed my gear and headed out the door. I had a good 50 miles to cover. Our Arlington crew was on its way to the scene with their patrol boat. 35-40 knot winds were blowing downriver in the area and the fetch allowed waves to build to considerable size. That is big enough to capsize a large tugboat. On the way up I was wondering just what we would be able to do to render assistance. I could hear radio traffic back and forth between those at the scene. Not being able to see what was going on or what the actual conditions were, I elected to stay out of the discussion.

I was on scene in a half hour and was struck by the intensity of the winds and the piling waves in the river. I drove over some dunes and contacted the local patrol Sergeant. Harold was in his car at the radio and motioned me over.

"Where's Mike?" I asked. Mike was our local Senior Trooper Game Officer and the one most adept at boat handling.

"Out there!" Harry answered, pointing to the middle of the river.

The tug was upside down and the barge he had been towing was drifting sideways.

"How many people in the water?" I asked.

"Three, maybe four. We haven't been able to locate them." He answered.

With binoculars I could see the 19 foot patrol boat pitching wildly into wave after wave in midriver.

"Who sent them out?" I asked again.

Harold replied, "District Headquarters ordered them to go. The Captain said the boat was more than adequate to handle 6-8 foot waves."

By this time I was getting really concerned. "I'm glad District can make that call from Bend. 100 miles away!" I answered sarcastically.

Mike was on the radio and advised us he was barely able to make headway and was in danger of capsizing. Plus they couldn't see anything floating and would not have been able to make a pickup in those conditions. He had to keep continuous power just to stay upright.

Coast Guard Units from Umatilla had responded with small rescue craft and confirmed my fears. That was no place for a small boat without specialized rescue capabilities. They weren't even going out until the chopper arrived.

I talked to Mike and asked him if he could work his way across the river to the Washington side. Turning back would have put him into dangerous broaching position. He agreed and advised us he was very close to less hazardous waters on the other side. I got into my patrol vehicle and headed for the bridge at Umatilla, 30 miles upriver. I crossed the bridge and headed back downriver toward the scene. I found Mike and the boat in a small cove. He had a relieved smile on his face. So did I. We stripped any equipment from the boat and tied it to the rocks so it would not batter itself overnight.

On the way back Mike related how nasty it really was out there. He said he was extremely concerned a few times.

In the meantime, the Coast Guard chopper picked one survivor out of the water. Two others perished and were not found for several days.

We got back to the scene on the Oregon side and I thanked Mike and told him I would be back the next day and we would get his boat back.

I got back to the office and told the Patrol Supervisor what had happened. Incredulously, all he was worried about was the boat we had left unattended for the night. I vowed to get to the bottom of the whole mess.

I wrote a report of the incident and as a result the policy was changed regarding the decision to go or not. It became the decision of the boat operator based on his experience, equipment and the conditions as he saw them. Everyone eventually agreed we had been extremely fortunate. The boat was retrieved in good shape the next day.

ON THE HUNT!

One of the most elusive guys on the river was Virgil. He always had the fastest boat. He would buy a ski boat hull and hang the biggest outboard he could find on the transom. One of the boats was so overpowered he had to fasten Styrofoam blocks to the transom so it would not sink when sitting still. Under full power it was a fire breathing streak of Fiberglas. Probably capable of 70 MPH plus!

Bob located a small dock near town one night with a fresh net piled neatly on top. We walked down to the site and set up surveillance. The rocks were warm and comfortable from the hot sun the previous day, even at 2:00AM.

We finally heard the boat approach from downriver. Virgil came to the dock and quickly loaded the net and raced off downriver again. Several hours later while it was still dark he came back. We had repositioned ourselves to be able to jump him at the dock.

We knew we could never catch him on the water. We were hiding behind some small bushes. Something alerted him and we froze in position. He continued to idle just inches from the dock staring in our direction. We didn't dare move and the standoff went on for 10-15 minutes. Suddenly he turned and headed off in the darkness downriver at top speed. We never saw him or his boat again on the river.

CAN'T ESCAPE THE LONG ARM OF THE LAW!

Another night we got a call from Washington fisheries of a skiff tied to the bushes near Wishram. Bob and I located a net near Rabbit Islands just across the river from the skiff and laid a plan. We would wait in our new jet sled in the bushes just upriver from the net. Agent Dave would alert us to any activity. USFWS was with us also.

About 0300 we received a call that the boat was on its way across the river. They came to the net and began pulling it into the boat. We couldn't see the boat but as soon as it started back we came blasting out of our hiding place with a 200HP motor at 5,000RPM. As it turned out they had a skiff with a 10 HP motor. Hardly enough to run from us!

We ran up behind the boat but they refused to stop. Elliot, a body builder, reached out and grabbed the transom of the fleeing boat. The puny 5 horse motor was no match for him. Those poor fishermen never had a chance! Captured by the long arm of the law!

Chapter VI

Salmon Scam

Salmon Scam as it came to be known, was hatched out of the need to protect the fishing rights of the legal tribal fishermen and stop the wholesale theft of thousands of fish from the Columbia River. It began after the officers from The Dalles, Hood River and Arlington took it upon themselves to prove to the powers that the fish were being decimated by a broken system.

For quite some time we had been questioning the requests for and documentation of early ceremonial fish permits. Managers were being duped by requests that authorized, for example, 5 nets for 5 days for 50 fish. These nets were set at pre arranged places and tended by tribal fishermen appointed by the tribes.

Our own officers, experienced with the nets, insisted these permits were far too liberal and were capable of taking much more than the authorized number of fish. Plans were put in place to stake out these sites and watch, document and compare the results with what was reported.

Immediately it was clear that perhaps hundreds of fish were being caught rather than 10-20 that were reported. In one case the actual take exceeded the authorized take by 400 fish! We had a pretty good idea these fish were being sold on the black market!

When we reported the discrepancy, we were challenged by the tribes and the managers for the State. We documented one case that involved the local sale of ceremonial fish to prove our point and the doors were opened.

I met with my Supervisor and Tribal Elders at Warm Springs and they requested we do what we could to curb the excesses. The Tribal leaders were displeased at the thought that ceremonial caught fish were being sold illegally! They insisted that we bring the guilty ones to justice so the law abiding fishermen could exercise their treaty rights.

The Captain called me several days later and asked what it would take to stop the illegal activities. I knew we would never get all we asked for so I quickly calculated what it would take to cover 60+ miles of river and shoreline 24 hours a day.

"Give me 25 men and 6 boats!" I hung up not expecting to hear back.

Several hours later I got the call. "You have them, now make it work!"

I was stunned and elated! Officers were brought in from other OSP offices, Idaho, USFWS, NMFS and ODFW. Now we had to lodge, assign and monitor activities. Washington in the meantime was gearing up on their side of the river to work with us.

In the meantime National Marine Fisheries Service was setting up an undercover operation. One of their Agents was placed in the mission and went into deep undercover living with Tribal Fishermen at Cook Landing and other locations. He established himself as an illegal buyer of fish with unlimited markets.

He and I met from time to time in the middle of the night in back alleys of The Dalles after making sure we were not being followed.

He relayed information that was vital to the safety of the Troopers and Agents working the day to day assignments. Little else could be passed on to the field for fear of Rich losing his cover.

That could have been fatal. He told me of several incidents that occurred when he was in the process of gaining their trust.

One night in a bar they demanded his wallet. He handed it over and they examined his cards and ID. Of course he was prepared for this, but one mistake and he may well have disappeared. These guys were not playing games.

He told me to pass on information to the field that traps for the officers were being discussed. One of them involved cutting the rattles off Rattlesnakes, common to the area and hanging them with string over paths we used to get to and from river bank observation sites.

We never found any of those nor did we find others he mentioned; nets with razor blades or barbed treble hooks twisted into the buoy lines. The thought of these kept us constantly alert, but even this information had to be kept quiet. They could have been feeding it to him it to blow his cover. It became a dangerous cat and mouse game.

*Author at work pulling an abandoned net full of
smelly rotten fish just off the mouth of the Deschutes River.
Interstate 84 in the background.*

Again we placed a huge amount of pressure on anyone suspected of illegal activity. The day to day presence of uniformed patrols took pressure off the undercover operation in that it gave the outlaws more to worry about. In addition we used plainclothes officers on the river posing as sport fishermen or just tourists. We were able to keep track of the suspects at all times.

One of the main fishermen the operation focused on was well known to all the officers on the river. Bruce was bold and outgoing with information. He would often tell us what he was going to do and where he was going to do it. We would caution him but he seemed to think he could operate with impunity. More than once we were waiting for him with citations ready to serve.

He and I had an informal eye to eye meeting one afternoon at the Celilo Park. This park is just off I84 and sits on the shore where Celilo Falls once roared with activity and gave up thousands of fresh Salmon yearly to the Tribal dip nets.

I had vivid memories of the falls from when I was a child when my Dad would stop and buy a fish.

Placid waters backed up by The Dalles Dam flow over Celilo Falls site. Once a beautiful set of rapids and churning waterfalls and a Tribal fishing site for thousands of years.

We talked about the days when we were kids and he told me how he was tied to the platforms so he would not fall in to the raging currents. He told me he was the grandson of the Chief.

I told him how my Dad had met the Chief and how highly respected he was. My Dad also told me about the inundation of the falls when they closed the dam at The Dalles backing up the river and silencing the roar. He was there when it happened.

Bruce seemed indifferent to my story like I was telling him something he already had heard from those most affected. But he listened politely anyway. I asked him why he insisted on defying the laws and paying the price.

He answered "You would never understand our ways."

"I'm trying," I replied.

We had sit down lunch meetings with the tribal fishermen as a means of diffusing any problems. Law enforcement had become a thorn in their side. Some of these meetings were cordial. Others ended with a touch of bitterness. We reminded them that we had entered into this agreement to strictly enforce the law at their request.

Regardless of their feelings it was our duty to enforce all State laws and if it upset them that was too bad. It was hard at times to maintain composure when they would fling racism charges at us after inviting us to come and talk. We bent over backwards at times to avoid riling them up.

I was always a firm believer in the Treaty of 1855. Many locals held the belief that we had somehow defeated the Tribes and "gave" those rights to fish. Quite the opposite was the truth. There were no wars during the settling of the river by the whites in the 1800s. Tribes retained their rights and actually gave rights to fish in common to the settlers.

At least that is what the Federal Courts interpreted. Fish were not considered a valuable commodity at the time by the settlers in any case. Only the tribes realized the full value of Salmon runs at that time. Non tribal fishermen would learn soon enough!

Still there were rules to be followed and most of the fishermen accepted that. Tribal Enforcement was just in its beginnings. They did not have the capability to cover the entire area. It was left to the States to manage and enforce the rules. And we never knew when State law would be trumped by Federal Treaty Laws.

Months went by and the pressure kept up. No one could move on the river without being checked by task force members.

It got to the point where activity slowed and became almost non existent. At least in the day time. There were more officers on the river than there were fishermen.

Once a Tribal boat was approached and a rifle came out. Before it could even be pointed at anyone, the shore line literally came alive as plainclothes officers stood up with assault rifles in hand! The fishermen meekly returned the rifle to its case and consented to inspection.

The operation went on for a year and with regular meetings in Portland it became evident that the undercover portion was so effective, NMFS Agent had become the major buyer of illegal fish on the river. It had to come to a halt.

Charges were prepared and citations written from cases that had been carefully documented in notebooks over the previous year. A massive takedown was put into effect. Dozens of tribal fishermen were cited to appear in court on hundreds of charges.

Three prominent tribal fishermen were arrested by Federal Officers and slated to appear in Federal Court. They were eventually found guilty and served 5 years in Federal Prison! More than 70 persons were cited or arrested. Nearly a hundred charges were filed on taking and selling some 50 tons of illegal fish.

June of 1982 the operation was ended and Officers returned to their homes and regular assignments.

The court proceedings drug on for a year with the majority of the cases consolidated and plea bargained. To prosecute every case would have clogged the entire local court system.

National human rights groups took up the cause and due to the plea wrangling were able to make it appear that once again the States and Federal Government ran roughshod over a few mostly "innocent" fishermen.

The operation was a success in that it solidified the need for Tribal enforcement on the river. Many of the officers involved felt the press painted them in an unfavorable light. They did what they were asked to do and did it effectively. The tribes that had begged that we arrest the outlaws and make it safe for the legal fishermen, now criticized our efforts and threw their support behind those who had stolen fish from them.

The men who were assigned to the river locally held their heads high and apologized to no one. I'm still proud of the way the operation was handled, documented and prosecuted.

The USFWS Agents and the NMFS Agents did an outstanding, professional and thorough job. It could not have been handled any better!

Five year prison sentences were handed down by the Federal District Court! That doesn't happen unless cases are properly investigated, prepared and executed.

After Salmon Scam faded from the screen, things got back to a quieter, normal, if you could call it that, way of life. Inter tribal Enforcement had been organized and taken over the majority of river enforcement. That left us to concentrate on other wildlife issues.

I missed the river work and began to get restless for a change. I was never particularly fond of working the hunting problems that plagued the area. I relied on the officers who were experts in that part of the job and was quite comfortable leaving them to their own clever devices.

NEVER IMPROVISE!

One incident though always left a bad taste in my mouth. During the Salmon Scam operation I asked Bob if he was willing to do the records and statistics. He was good at it and I saw a chance to use his skills. I reported this at one of the meetings in Portland and a Captain seemed annoyed that a Senior Trooper was "put in charge" of a project. He felt that was the province of Sergeants! That somehow I wasn't doing my part!

Some time later one of my District supervisors came up and rode with me on patrol. I could tell something was eating at him so I finally asked him. He said he had come up to find out why I had used a Trooper in a position of responsibility. I told him I felt Bob was the best man for the job. I know headquarters felt I had overstepped. That I had the nerve to try something without approval from the higher ups!

After 8 years of fighting local commanders who seemed to have little grasp of how wildlife enforcement worked I put in for and was given a new assignment as District Sergeant at Portland Headquarters. I plunged headlong into the new assignment and was now working for a Fish and Game Lieutenant who actually understood the job and appreciated the work we were doing!

Several years after I had transferred out of The Dalles to Portland, General Headquarters came down with a "new" idea. We were going to empower Senior Troopers to perform tasks of responsibility that had previously been given to Sergeants and above.

They were all patting themselves on the back and telling us what a great idea it was! I thought so too!

Chapter VII

The Sport Fleet

Often we tend to focus on one side of wildlife violations. Rest assured that while hundreds of hours were spent chasing fishing violations, equal time was spent on angling violations. In Oregon the legal definition of fishing is any means used to capture fish other than hook and line. Gaffing, spearing, clubbing, netting are all "fishing" violations.

Many so called "sport anglers" had become adept at using illegal means to capture fish while using sport gear. It was a standing practice, as soon as the new angling rules came out, these sports would look for the loopholes. Their only goal in practicing angling was to see how many or how big of fish they could take.

Gillnet fishermen did not have a monopoly on harvesting fish for the illegal markets. It was just the fact that a good outlaw gill netter with the right gear could devastate many fish in a short period of time.

Tuning patrol techniques to catch anglers required different approaches to the problem. Most angling violations occurred during daylight hours. With hundreds of boats on the water at one time in a given area it was often difficult to pick out the culls from the legitimate angler.

Again, surveillance was a valuable tool. Watching a known group of anglers from a vantage point, logging information as it occurred and then later contact to verify what was seen and issuing citations as needed.

PRESCOTT BEACH

On the lower Columbia there were plunking areas where groups of anglers camped on the beach and set up tents and travel trailers for the duration of the season. Our nightly patrols included running slowly past these areas as close as possible to the shore without running aground.

The common practice was to cast their lines out and let the lure sink to the bottom with weight attached. They would then attach a bell, put the rod in a holder and settle back till the bell rang, signaling a bite. This method was as effective in the dark as it was in the daylight. However fishing after dark was illegal.

As we cruised along the shoreline we would snag their line and the bell would ring. They would tumble out of their sleeping bags and expecting a fish, set the hook. Only then would they realize that somewhere out there in the dark was a rather large patrol boat with rather large officers that enjoyed writing citations!

When the Salmon season closed early and Steelhead remained open it was not unusual for the plunkers to catch

Salmon while angling for Steelhead. The dishonest kept the salmon, hid them in their rigs or buried them in the sand till it was time to leave.

I guess they thought we had never heard of their tactics. They were usually wrong! Their pretend surprise when we started to dig salmon up near their feet was comical! Usually their wives blurted out information sinking them even deeper, or one of their little kids couldn't resist bragging on poor old Dad.

ONLY HARD CORE POACHERS COULD LIE WITH A STRAIGHT FACE.

One Officer I will never forget was Sgt. Gary Suhaldonik. He worked for Washington Game Department and spent most of his career in the Longview area where I first met him. He had a great sense of humor as well as a firm grasp of the law. We were running boat patrols during the Spring Chinook run and every time we passed on beach on Puget Island the bank anglers would give us the one finger salute, knowing we could not come onto Washington soil and check them. A visual check from the boat told us there were quite a few more rods fishing than there were people. Anglers in both states are limited to one rod per person.

I called Gary and told him what we were seeing. He asked us to pick him up the next day. We welcomed him aboard upriver and continued down toward Puget Island.

As we approached the salutes came out once again. We headed the boat toward the beach and landed in the middle of the plunkers. At first they were yelling and telling us we had no authority on their side.

Gary just stepped out onto the beach and ordered the fishermen to stand at their rods. "And I don't want to see any cut lines or reeling in." Gary admonished.

It soon became obvious there were far more rods fishing than people. Gary gathered up the extra rods and asked if anyone wanted to claim them. A couple did and received citations, but he ended up seizing more than a dozen rods. From then on we either got no salutes from the beach or just friendly waves as we passed by.

Gary and I became friends and often called each other in the middle of the night, especially after Oregon Ducks vs. Washington Husky football games. If Washington won he would bark in the phone and hang up. If the Ducks won I would quack in the phone and hang up. In those years Gary got to bark a lot more than I got to quack. Gary was really one of the good guys!

I learned from a wise old officer who trained me that you never wanted to take violations personally. If you did the job would drive you nuts! The stupidest thing a game violator does is justify his actions by thinking he is either outsmarting the officer or getting even! And some of them went so far as to brag about it.

One violator, after we caught him with too many fish, blurted out his revenge statement". You'll pay for this one! I'm going to go out and poach the biggest Bull Elk I can find."

I looked at him and smiled, "Son. You better hope that no elk get poached in this area for the next 2 years. Because if they do, you are going to be the prime suspect! "

He backed off and tried to convince us he was only joking.

"Nope, you made the statement! You are on the list!" I replied. "And you, killing an elk, is not going to cost me anything!"

The great majority of licensed fishermen appreciate the job enforcement does. They know the wildlife belongs to them and they are paying us to protect it. Regrettably thieves often don't see it that way.

Recently in the Northwest sporting groups of organized hunters and anglers have set up TIP programs and rewards for information leading to convictions of game thieves. Anglers are quick to spot people exceeding the bag limit, snagging Salmon or keeping wild fish. Cell phones are common equipment and they are not afraid to use them. Most of the time, Fish and Wildlife Officers prefer to think of sportsmen as honest, law abiding people out for a good time. In most cases they are and even though suspicions arise there is little proof and you begin second guessing your suspicions. I know I did when I first began working at the St. Helens Office in the 70s.

Recently fishing with and visiting with old timers who were in their younger days as I was, I have been made aware of the reality of suspected illegal practices that permeated the sport fishery while I was there.

Some of the more "eager" violators who probably considered themselves to be "smarter" than the cops went to extreme means to catch more fish than was legal or to hide those fish when the game wardens approached.

Just as we suspected but could not always prove due to constitutional restraints and simply being outnumbered and over whelmed by the number of sportsmen, I have confirmed since the practices of hanging stringers of fish on anchor ropes, under false floorboards, buried in the sand and the disposal of excess fish through of all places, restaurants! Who would have thought?

It is ironic that these same sportsmen now suffer the loss of once magnificent fish runs and can only blame the commercial fishermen for over harvest! Or the Wildlife Departments for mismanaging the runs.

I recall talking to a group of old timers at a boat ramp in Tillamook about the good old days when they used to snag salmon at night with pitchforks by the gunnysack or toss a gillnet into the stream behind their homes and haul in twenty fish a night. "How come the fish aren't running like that anymore?" They ask.

"Golly I don't have the slightest idea!" I replied. All the while trying to avoid telling them what I was really thinking.

Truthfully, one poacher is not going to kill off the entire run and there are a myriad of reasons from dams, to habitat that contribute to the problem. But someone wisely noted once that if you are not part of the solution, you are then part of the problem.

BLACK POINT!

An extensive operation was set up some years ago at a notorious spot below Oregon City Falls. Spring Chinook fishermen there formed a tight knit group and apparently tried to break every law on the books. Officers rotated in and out of a surveillance spot and watched the anglers take excessive numbers of fish day in and day out. The violators made a habit of changing hats and shirts as a weak attempt to foil observers. After several weeks of gathering info the entire group was contacted simultaneously and had their tags checked against the officer's notes and photographs. Roughly 12 fishermen were cited for 30 or more counts of exceeding and failing to tag fish.

One of the fishermen was a school official. He was cited and called me to complain about the tactics used by the officers. He felt he was publicly embarrassed and only went along in the group because they were his friends.

I reminded him of an old saying. "Roll around in the mud with pigs and you will get muddy!"

Lawful sportsmen expressed their appreciation to the officers for cleaning that mess up. Years later it still comes up in conversations.

NOT MY FISH!

Humor often crept into sport violations also. I was working the docks on the ocean fishery at Garibaldi one year and one of the fish checkers employed by ODFW contacted me and pointed out a large Salmon hanging on a scale. A guide had brought the fish in and onlookers were admiring it for its size. The only problem was that it was a wild Coho! They are not legal to keep.

I pointed the error out to the guide who suddenly realized his mistake! He and everyone else thought it was a Chinook due to its size.

He walked off down the dock and I followed. "I'm going to issue a citation for the fish." I told him.

"I didn't catch it, my mother did." He replied.

"So you're going to let your mother get cited?" I asked almost knowing the answer.

"Yup it's her fish, her ticket."

WHAT I THOUGHT I SAW

Shortly after I moved to Portland I was invited to join a friend at Tillamook for some fall Salmon fishing. Dan was one of the best spinner fishermen I had ever met and fun to fish with. We had a great day boating 7 prime fall Chinook in the shallow water of the upper bay. We out fished every other boat that day and I went home tired and satisfied.

The next day at work we got a report from dispatch of illegal tactics and exceeding at Tillamook the day before. I was reading the description of the boat and its occupants when I realized it was our boat! The person who turned us in was convinced that no one could catch that many Salmon without foul hooking them and he was adamant we had taken at least 12 fish!

I contacted him by phone and listened to his description of what he had seen. It was obvious soon enough that he did not appreciate us out fishing him and his group. When he finished I politely explained to him that what he saw was really not what had taken place. His story came apart in bits and pieces and he became very apologetic. I explained to him that we really appreciated calls like his and that many investigations turned out just the way this one had. Every story has two sides.

I KNOW A COP WHEN I SEE ONE!

Early in my wildlife career the older officer who was training me took me to Eagle Creek to work snaggers. Chinook and Silvers were stacked up in one hole and the locals were having a great time. No one knew me yet so I put on my camo gear over my uniform, grabbed my spinning rod and headed for the hole. Clyde went to the opposite side and hid in the brush where he could see.

I began casting and while retrieving accidentally snagged a Silver.

I jerked to release the hook and one of the perps yelled "fish on!" And then he came over to help.

The fish got off and he started yapping about how I messed up. So he showed me how to snag a fish and yard it in to shore. I acted as interested as I could and he then offered me a joint.

"Nope", I replied, "I don't touch the stuff!"

"Hey there are no cops around, I can spot 'em from a mile away." he boasted.

I went on casting for awhile and then noticed Clyde coming down the trail. We had watched this guy and two others land and keep snagged fish.

The guy moved over near me and whispered, "I think that's a cop coming. Act legal"

I smiled and opened my jacket showing him my badge. He jumped back and turned pale.

"I knew you were a cop!" he kept repeating.

I laughed and said, "If you knew I was a cop, why did you offer me a joint?"

He just moaned and gave up. This job was fun and I was getting paid to do it! Sometimes it was too easy, or poachers are just plain ignorant!

BOAT RAMP HOLE

Pacific City was another hot spot for illegal activity. The boat ramp hole on the Nestucca was downright dirty with snaggers in the fall. The Lieutenant requested some volunteers to go fish the hole and try to slow the snagging down.

I volunteered and headed over the mountains. The boat ramp hole was right in the middle of town at where else? The boat ramp! I had my own vehicle and thought I could blend in. In the 70s, short hair and a clean shaven face meant one thing. They made me as a cop before I could settle in and most of them wandered off or went legal.

In the 90s I had an occasion to return to Pacific City. I drove down in an unmarked vehicle and even though I was cleanly dressed and shaven no one paid any attention to me.

I acted like a tourist and asked dumb questions like, "What are you fishing for?" "What kinds of Salmon run here?"

One gentleman was talking to me and explained how this used to be a bad place but most of the anglers now followed the rules. He pointed out one young kid who was putting the jerk in the retrieve. "Now there's a snagger."

About that time the kid laid into one and drug it in close enough to see the spinner in its side. He was bearing down so hard I thought the rod was going to snap. One of the other fishermen told him to release the fish. "We don't want any cops down here!"

The kid waded out and unhooked the fish. It rolled on its side exhausted and just as I was going to say something, another angler screamed at him. "Get out there and release that fish right, Damn it!"

The kid jumped and grabbed the fish and carefully revived it then released it to swim off, then meekly returned to his spot on the shore.

I chuckled at the reaction of the fishermen and the gentleman I was talking to looked at me quizzically.

"You don't suppose there was a cop watching do you?" he asked.

"You bet your sweet ass there was!" I replied. "Thanks guys."

I thought the guy was going to bust a gut laughing as I walked off. "Thank you!" he yelled back at me. "Come on back anytime!" What a change!

OFFSHORE PATROL

I learned how to navigate the Columbia River Bar when I was assigned to work the offshore sport fishery. On busy weekends I took our patrol boat to Astoria worked with another officer. We would contact boats on the ocean, jump aboard and check their licenses and tags. Wayne and I had a system worked out. I would maneuver the boat close to another boat, he would jump over and I would back off and wait. He boarded a rather nice cruiser with two couples on board and I could see he had detected a violation. Generally we cited one spouse even if both had violated the law.

Wayne wrote one ticket then went from one to the other and kept writing. He finally gave me the high sign so I pulled alongside and picked him up.

"What was that all about?" I asked. He was pretty angry and said they all had barbed hooks and none had validated their tags. "I was just going to write the men when one of the women called me a pig!"

"That did it!", he exclaimed.

"What the hell are you laughing at?" Wayne asked as he looked at me.

"Nothing! "I could hardly contain myself.

People constantly talked themselves into tickets. One of the hardest things an officer does is write a citation to a polite person. One of the easiest and most satisfying things an officer does is write a citation to a jerk. It pays to be nice!

We often put in 10-12 hour days during the busy season. There was no provision for overtime with OSP in those days. The higher ups told us it was voluntary but expected. When evaluation time rolled around the "voluntary hours" meant a passing or improving performance rating.

We compensated for that when we could. Ocean patrols were opportune times to sneak some sport gear onboard the patrol boats and then when out of sight of land and the fleet, we would catch our limits of fresh salmon, hide them in the boat and return to port.

Supervisors were always looking; it seemed, to find some evidence of what they considered foul play. There was nothing illegal about it just was against Department procedure. Our supervisor was a large man, but had a great heart; I think he always knew when we had been "off the clock" so to speak. He couldn't get into some of the small spaces in the boat but would be quick to spot a spot of fish blood on our gear.

"Be careful!" He would caution with a smile.

PERMISSION TO BOARD?

No officer goes through his career without losing his cool once or twice. I was working the off shore dory fishery at Pacific City one year late in my career. I was jumping boats and as we pulled alongside one boat operated by a lady, I started over the side. Just as I put one leg over the Zodiac a small shark about 5 feet long jumped at my leg and brushed against it. It startled me and I leapt into the dory with both feet planted firmly on the deck.

The lady Captain yelled at me and told her deckhand to throw me over the side. Now there is no way that skinny little dude was going to dump me over the side without him going with me and I let them know that! She lit into me about boarding without permission, blah, blah, her boat, she was Captain! I was unimpressed and told her so in not so polite terms! I climbed back aboard the Zodiac and we left that contact.

She wrote the Governor, the Governor wrote the OSP and my Captain called me in for a counseling session. I explained the details. He totally grasped the situation, laughed about it and told me I was to consider myself disciplined and case closed. He replied to the Governor that I had been given counseling and the matter had been taken care of.

Some ten years after I retired I came back to work as a part time enforcement officer for the summer at Pacific City of all places! I was again checking dories as they landed on the beach.

A very familiar lady was operating one of them and commented while I was checking that she was one of the original Captains of the fleet.

I thought to myself, "This is deja vu all over again!"

She said "surely you've had heard of me."

She went on to recount the story of how this officer jumped her boat and defied her. Her version had me suspended, demoted and sent to school to get rehabilitated.

I 'fessed up that I was the one and in reality nothing like that had happened. "Sorry to disappoint you Captain." As I tipped my hat and walked away.

THE BRITISH ARE COMING!

Often we worked plainclothes in unmarked boats just trying to stay ahead of the hard core violators at Oregon City. One young man knew us by sight and every time we got on the water he ran from boat to boat telling everyone we were coming. We called him Paul Revere.

I was sitting on a bluff one spring observing the fishery below with a spotting scope when I noticed an older man in a boat by himself land a fish. Then he landed a second one and kept fishing. He was going to exceed right before my eyes! I snuck down off the bluff, got in my truck with the boat all ready to launch and headed for the ramp.

I headed the boat upriver and spotted the guy still sitting in the same spot. Just then "Paul Revere" came by and went right to the boat and pointed to me.

I pulled up and identified myself. "Move over Paul." I said.

The older guy was kind of miffed and told me that was his son and his name was not Paul.

"I know, but that's what we call him." I explained. He looked a little puzzled as I asked to see his two fish. Neither of them were tagged.

I explained to him that normally I might issue a warning for failure to tag but in his case I was going to make an exception. I went on to explain how his son seemed to consider it his duty to warn all the other anglers of our presence and I wanted to return the favor.

As I handed him his citation to appear in court I said, "don't thank me, thank your son" Funny how things worked out at times.

TURN THAT LIGHT OFF!

The mouth of the Clackamas had a special hog line that seemed to have a habit of committing violations. They were a close knit group and kept watch for each other.

Early one morning before legal fishing hours, Lloyd was on shore and heard voices from the boats tied on anchor. He figured they were probably fishing but there was no way to tell in the dark. One boat dropped off anchor and headed for the ramp.

Lloyd was always thinking ahead. He met the boat and told the operator to keep quiet and take him back out to the others. The guy reluctantly agreed and they pushed off. As they neared the line Lloyd lit them up with his flashlight, noting lines already in the water.

"Turn the damn light off idiot! The cops might see us!" came from the other boats.

"Yup." Lloyd replied, "They might! Here's your ticket!"

Chapter VIII

Gravel to Gravel

After transferring from The Dalles, the lower river became my focus once again. Most of the old outlaws were gone but so were the fish. We had to come up with plans that addressed habitat concerns and allocation issues.

There was little or no Sport fishing left on the Spring Salmon runs. Counts had fallen to less than 100,000 fish over Bonneville and once abundant Sockeye runs diminished to 2 fish at one point.

Tributaries of the Willamette River and the Willamette itself became the priority. We still had fishable runs in the Willamette and we were determined to save them.

ANYBODY NEED A RIDE?

One spring night on Eagle Creek a secondary tributary of the Willamette/ Clackamas system, Lloyd, one of the Senior Officers out of the Portland office was checking the banks on foot.

He had hidden his patrol vehicle and noticed a pickup driving slowly down the road like he was looking for someone. He saw a figure run out of the brush, toss a gunny sack in the back and return to the river. Lloyd waited till the truck approached again and flagged it down.

He recognized the driver as one of an ethnic group that frequented the area and harvested more than their share of fish. Lloyd identified himself and told the driver to move over and keep quiet. Lloyd then took the wheel and began his trip down the road and back slowly looking for more poachers.

It was pitch back out and raining so visibility was in his favor. Several more perps came out of the brush and jumped in the back of the truck with their bags of freshly caught illegal salmon.

Now Lloyd is a quick thinker and he knew he had to put himself in a position to nab all the bad guys at once. Once he figured he had the whole group he drove on down the road to an open area, stopped, jumped out and identified himself. Several of them jumped off and ran for the brush. They escaped but several others were cited and then released.

Lloyd made sure they left the area and followed them down the main road. The ones left in the brush were in for a long walk and a wet cold night! He warned the driver and his companions that they had better go home and not return that night.

When we reported the case at the staff meeting the following week, our Commanding Officer winced but admitted it was a case of the officer thinking on his feet and improvising.

OOPS, WRONG GUY!

Other officers developed information of a small time drug dealer in SE Portland who was rumored to be netting the Willamette River near Wheatland downstream from Salem. A drive by of his residence told us he had the necessary gear. Several old gill nets were heaped up near the garage and an old skiff was sitting on a trailer.

We set up surveillance of the only realistic route to the area and spent several weeks waiting for him to move. In the meantime, local officers from the McMinnville Office put the river sled on the water and waited. Grand Island is a small island just off the Willamette River and was home to several vegetable and fruit farms.

One night after sitting on the roadway and the river for hours the officers decided to call it quits. On the way back upriver just off Grand Island they nearly ran into a small gill net. Quickly they backed off and set up observation. Just before daylight a man walked down to the water, launched a small boat and pulled the net full of bright Spring Chinook.

He was easily apprehended and lived on the island. He was arrested and the fish, net and boat seized. He was not the one we had spent all the time watching and waiting for. He was just a local getting more than his share of fish. In spite of our efforts the other suspect never showed up or gave us any indication he was going to. We took what was available at the time and called it good.

Spring Chinook Salmon seized after fisherman was caught near Wheatland Ferry on the Willamette River.

Gravel to gravel was a name we gave to the ongoing operation in the tributaries. Salmon are hatched and live out of the gravel then go to sea and return to the gravel where they were born. We wanted to make that process as successful as we could for the remainder of the fish.

Bonneville Power Administration had a stake in the recovery of the salmon. Their operation was dependent upon generating power with the water that passed thru the dams. The better the fish runs the more water they could use for the turbines. They heavily subsidized our enforcement operations with equipment and overtime hours. For once we had the tools to do the job, but was it too late for the fish?

Columbia River Spring Chinook fishing had come to a standstill and this enabled us to concentrate our efforts on specific sites. One of them was the old fish station at Mayger that had fallen into shambles.

BPA funding had supplied us with a mobile observation vehicle equipped with black and white and color video zoom cameras. Two people could literally live inside the van and observe without ever being detected. The van had listening devices on each corner and a self activated alarm system in case anyone tried to get inside.

We used it to set up across the river from Mayger and began watching. Zooming in we began to see what was a small fishing operation with hand lines and lures. These guys knew what they were doing and were very successful at hooking Spring Chinook and moving them into one the abandoned buildings nearby.

Once we were satisfied they had taken enough of the fish from the river we moved in with search warrants. We identified the persons who had caught the fish from the recorded video. Faced with evidence on tape they told us why they were catching the fish. It seemed there was a fireman's picnic scheduled for later in the month in Longview. Grilled salmon was on the menu!

"Sorry guys that is not an excuse for poaching salmon!"

One of the fishermen apparently thought he could toss a wrench into our machinery. He produced a sport salmon tag with several fish marked as caught in the Willamette River which was open. We politely asked him if he really wanted to testify in court, under oath, that he had taken those fish legally. He quickly changed his mind and put the tag back in his pocket. The arrests made the newspaper in Longview and word spread about the hazards of even small scale poaching.

Even as I was winding down to my retirement I had a feeling of sadness that I was leaving a job at a time when the fish were in serious trouble. Not that I could do much about it. The problems were far flung and very complicated. I had always lived with the belief that anyone is replaceable. There were people waiting to fill my position.

PLATFORMS AND DIPNETS

The spring before my retirement we got word that the Tribal fishermen were going to leave their traditional fishing grounds above Bonneville and claim fishing rights at their ancestral grounds. Namely Oregon City Falls!

Meetings were scheduled and the plans for enforcement action were discussed. I knew from past cases this would be an exercise in futility to resist the effort. Some of the Administrators from Salem expressed the desire to arrest the Tribal Fishermen and haul them to jail. I wanted no part of that!

I was close enough to retirement I was going to get my way or else! I asked them if they wanted to come up and take over my job. They agreed to let us handle it our way.

The event was heavily covered by the media and they were set up to film and cover another confrontation. I assured them it was not going to happen. The only thing they would see would be the issuance of citations. The courts would decide their fate. Some of the reporters seemed disappointed at that news. We put our patrol boat in the water and went across the river to watch. The tribal fishermen built a scaffold just like the ones that used to straddle Celilo Falls on the Columbia. When they finished they took up their nets and made a ceremonial dip. We went across the river with the boat and issued each fisherman a citation, gave them instructions and the event was over.

We went back to our boat and one of the younger officers pointed out one of the Tribal members standing high on the rocks screaming at us. I told him to go see what he wanted.

Vic went up and talked to the man and came back smiling." He's pissed because he didn't get a ticket!" He wants to be part of the protest.

"Hell, oblige him." I said, "But tell him he has to put his net in the water first."

Vic went back watched the man dip his net and issued the citation. The guy was grinning from ear to ear! He was now a part of history!

A week later the courts dismissed the citations and the scaffolds were dismantled. They had proven their point and I was secretly glad they did. All the tribes wanted were to be recognized as the first fishermen on the waters. Most of their historic grounds were flooded by hydro dams. Dams that were once described to us in Police Academy by Captain Larson as "Monuments to the stupidity of mankind!"

Chapter IX

The Albemarle

Now retirement was really looming closer! Trying to identify problem areas and keep the river patrols busy with productive work was challenging. We were given a 28 foot sport fishing boat by the Feds who had seized it in a drug operation. It was a classy looking lady with twin engines and outriggers. We decided to make a summer trip upriver as a floating undercover platform and see what we could see.

I started the trip from Astoria with local officers and the plan was to replenish the crew every couple days on the trip to the Snake River. I was going to stay on the boat all the way.

The lower river was quiet and uneventful save for a bikini movie shoot on the beaches of Sauvie Island. We had to observe that no illegal activity was taking place and proceeded upriver!

We spent the night in Portland and the next day with a new crew headed for the Upper River. We locked through Bonneville Dam and were scheduled to spend the night in

Hood River. I had the Sergeant there arrange for moorage and I was going to spend the night on the boat.

We got to the moorage later that afternoon and discovered we were tying up at the County dock. I raised some opposition as I did not want to compromise the undercover status of the boat but was assured that everything had been taken care of.

The officers went home and I settled back to enjoy the sun in my shorts and tee shirt looking as much like any other tourist as I could. I turned on the stereo and watched the other people moving around the marina. Several people came over and admired the boat. It was turning out to be a beautiful evening!

Some time later a young Deputy came strolling up, placed his hands on his hips and with all the authority he could muster, declared, "Move that boat, now!"

At first I thought he was joking and knew it was an undercover boat. I laughed, "That's not going to happen!" I eyed him waiting for his next reply.

Again he said, "Move that boat before I put a hole in it!"

"What?" I replied, now realizing he was not joking. I became very defensive, motioned him to come closer. I told him I was with OSP and this was an undercover boat.

To my complete amazement he replied, "This is not an undercover boat and you aren't a cop! Now move the boat mister!"

I was now beginning to get mad, first because the Deputy was acting like a jerk and second he didn't believe me! He made a move toward the boat.

I said, "Don't touch my boat. He stepped back hesitating and again I said, "Get away from my boat!"

I picked up my cell phone and dialed the local Sergeant. The Deputy retreated to his vehicle. I could see him looking at me through his binoculars. The Sergeant answered the phone and I told him what had happened. At first he didn't believe it. I was not in a good mood and reminded him of our conversation about the moorage spot.

He assured me he would call me back. Shortly he called and told me the Sheriff was on his way down. I had known the Sheriff for years and he was one of the old good guys. But I was still in doubt how this was going to play out.

I motioned to the Deputy to come down to the boat. He cautiously approached and I said, "For your sake we should straighten this out before the Sheriff gets here."

He simply replied, "I told you to move the boat and I mean it!"

I was no longer in any mood to discuss it so I threw up my hands, settled back and waited. The Deputy was nervously pacing the dock unsure of what he should do.

A few minutes later the Sheriff arrived with his under sheriff.

I said, "Hello Joe, good to see you again!"

He asked, "What the hell is going on here?"

I explained the whole incident while the Deputy stood there and said nothing. I told him how I had my doubts about mooring the boat there in the first place. He and his assistant walked down the dock with the Deputy between them and I could tell from the body language it was not going well for the young man.

They returned and Joe told me I had two choices, I was welcome to leave the boat where it was or move it to another slip and the Deputy would help me. I told him under the circumstances I preferred to move the boat. I wanted to get as far away as possible.

The Sheriff apologized to me for the incident. They left; I untied the boat and moved it to another slip with the able assistance of the Deputy. When it was secure the Deputy came up shook my hand and said, "I'm supposed to apologize to you but I really don't know why."

I said quietly, "Young man, I hope someday you will understand." He headed back to the boathouse and disappeared.

I sat there for a while going over in my mind over what had happened and what I could have done differently. Did I over react? It occurred to me that I really didn't have to do this one last project. My fervor for the assignment was no longer there.

I called my wife and said, "Come and get me, I'm done. I'll explain it when you get here." We lived 60 miles away.

I had less than two months to go and had plenty of vacation time saved. I called the Sergeant and told him to find another boat operator.

My wife picked me up an hour later and took me home. She was amused and amazed at the story I told her.

My last confrontation of my career had been with a well meaning but badly inexperienced fellow officer of the law. How ironic! I often wonder how his career progressed. I wish him only the best. I'm sure he thought he was just doing his job. I finished up some waiting paperwork, spent some time in the office and retired for good on September 30, 1994, or so I thought.

Chapter X

Almost Busted!

After retirement I had the chance to fulfill another lifelong dream. Own a fishing lodge and charter business in Alaska with a partner. We started on a shoestring with a Lodge that was severely neglected. We brought several boats up and a friend also brought his boat to spend the summer with us and fish along with helping out.

So there we were in Clam Gulch with three boats in the yard and fishing every day. We took all of our friends fishing and while I had plans to guide I had not secured my Coast Guard license yet. The last thing I wanted to was to put my business at risk by doing something illegal! Someone apparently thought otherwise.

One day I returned from fishing and my wife met me in the yard. She pointed out a black Ford Bronco with several antennas parked in the yard. It fairly screamed LAW ENFORCEMENT! She said two guys made reservations to stay and wanted to go fishing. To her, something just didn't look right.

I met them and we talked about the boats and the fishing. They immediately asked to be taken on a guided fishing trip. I politely explained that I was not licensed and we only went on pleasure trips.

"But we'll pay for it!" the bigger guy insisted.

I declined again. My longtime Law Enforcement experience told me to go easy.

His friend was dressed in jungle fatigues and combat boots and sported very short hair. I knew something was up but figured I would let it play out. I knew we were legal and had nothing to worry about.

We spent the evening talking. The big guy said he was a banker from Anchorage. Naturally the subjects were fishing and hunting. I let him do most of the talking and reveal as much about himself as possible. He knew more about wildlife laws than any banker I had ever met.

The next morning the three of us were having breakfast. He leaned over and quietly asked what it would take to get a guided trip. I was ready!

I said "You want to go fishing with me? Let's go. But it's on me. I can't charge a cent even for gas but I like you guys!"

He acted a little surprised then turned to his partner and said, "Dang it, I just remembered. I have a meeting at noon! We have to get back to Anchorage!"

They both feigned disappointment and thanked us for our hospitality and left.

My wife came in and asked, "What was that all about?"

"Oh nothing, just a case of misguided suspicions." I replied.

I explained to her how her instincts were right on. These guys were on a different kind of fishing expedition. We had just been the focus of an undercover investigation! But having been there myself I held no ill feelings about the incident. You win some and you lose some!

I took the checkbook and made a trip into town to the Fish and Wildlife Department in Soldotna. I asked to see whoever was in charge of law enforcement. I related the story to her and offered to show her our checkbook and the thousands of dollars worth of fishing trips we had booked for our clients with licensed guides. She seemed unconcerned and claimed no knowledge of the investigation.

They were nice guys but as I told a Fish and Game supervisor later. "You have to do a better job of acting if you want to catch bad guys!"

She said, "I have no idea of what you are talking about."

"Of course." I replied, "Of course."

A year later I got my Master Coast Guard license and began guiding. One local officer commented, "Nice to see you got legal."

"I have no idea what you are talking about." I replied with a grin.

A couple of years later I volunteered to instruct some new park rangers working the Kenai river on covert tactics and how to work illegal guides effectively. Number one on the list, I told them, act dumb and let them do the talking. In other words let the person show you how they violate the laws and get away with it.

Chapter XI

Return to Oregon

6 years in Alaska was all my dear wife could tolerate. She had given in to my impulse and I will be forever indebted to her. It was everything I could have imagined. Grizzly Bears in the yard, Moose with calves coming to the door, Bald Eagles nearly eating out of my hand and hundreds of big fish. Sitting on anchor with whales circling the boat, running home from 15 miles offshore with a storm chasing us all the way. Many new friends and a lifetime of memories!

Still it was good to get back to Oregon. We settled in Tillamook at first and after a few years working seasonal jobs with OSP, we moved back to the Lower Columbia where I had started my career. Now we were closer to the Grandchildren and old friends and the opportunity to continue working Fish and Game part time in the fall.

While working out of Tillamook I had occasion to work one of the larger charter boat disasters ever to occur on the Oregon coast. The Taki Too broached and sank on June 3, 2003 with the loss of 11 lives including the Skipper. This was a collection of thoughts I wrote the next day. A day I will never forget.

When I got up yesterday morning, I had every intention of signing on at 7:00AM and going to Barview as I did usually every other day before work and watching the bar. I had no idea of what was unfolding at the time. I decided instead to have breakfast and signed on at 8:15 AM. By then all hell had broken loose at the North Jetty of Tillamook Bay. I was advised to get to the area as quickly as possible and render any aid necessary.

I arrived shortly at Barview and was immediately put to work aiding rescuers who were transporting victims, everyone up to their shoulders in work. My assignment was to keep onlookers off the beach area. The Taki was on it's side out in the surf. Rescue swimmers from the Coast Guard were getting hammered by huge waves as they hung onto their precious cargo. God Bless them and keep them safe!

The media had not yet arrived and when they did the gravitated to our position. I am no stranger to TV cameras but when they began asking for interviews, I somehow felt I had not yet paid my dues on this one. I had worked car crashes, plane crashes, and boat accidents but this one was different. We pointed out a young couple who had assisted survivors ashore and were sitting there quietly watching the proceedings. They readily answered questions and it was obvious they had been deeply affected by the events. Their answers came from within with no prompting or coaching. I was impressed by their forthrightness and confidence in the face of the cameras. I've seen professionals flush and go blank under lesser conditions.

The media was unusually respectful of the people involved and went out of their way to accommodate. They respected the boundaries we set up and went about their business.

One young man came down to the approach and asked if he could go look at the boat. He said he was supposed to have gone on the Taki and arrived just as they were about to leave the dock.

Two seats were left. One on the Taki and one on the D&D. A man he had never met wanted theTaki and he went on the D&D. He watched in awe later as the Taki broached and rolled over in the surf.

His wife and infant had stayed on shore and she thought he was on the Taki. She ran to the beach looking for him among the survivors and could not get him on the cell phone. He could not hear his phone because the ocean was so rough. He said he knew someone was looking out for him. As he walked back to his car, I wished him a Happy Father's Day!

A group of people holding hands approached and asked if they could walk down to the wreckage. I said no and one of them said he had been on the Taki with his Dad and he did not survive. We waved them through. As they walked down the beach, they stood in the shallow surf and held hands as if praying. They gathered at the boat briefly and came back up the beach. They smiled and waved at us as they passed.

An AP reporter asked me who they were. I hesitated then told him. He started toward them and then came back. He said he just could not invade their privacy right then. I thanked him.

I watched the 47 foot Coast Guard rescue boat bob in the surf, it's stern pitching high as it's bow as it rocked in the wild surf. The crew sat at their positions as if on a carnival ride.

Brave men! The helo plucked a victim from the surf right in front of us and the swimmer, dangling from the cable braved huge waves as he held tight to his precious cargo. The sea was not going to get it back!

I thought about all the boat tragedies and memorials to those who perished in rescues and commercial fishermen who perished at sea. But has there been a memorial to those innocents who bought their ticket to a day of fishing and never returned home? There should be.

Today I went to work, drove south to Pacific City and went to a high point at the mouth of the Nestucca where I could see 20 miles out to sea. A 47 foot Coast Guard boat was heading south on a smooth sea. I turned on the VHF radio to listen for traffic. "Pan Pan, Pan Pan, this is the U.S. Coast Guard Station Tillamook. After a sad day at Tillamook Bay the U.S. Coast Guard is suspending the search for the missing of the Taki Too, pending further developments. This is U.S. Coast Guard Tillamook out.

The scanner went dead silent for several minutes.

I turned to a music station on FM and went on patrol.

The last stanza from Tennyson's "Crossing the Bar" played in my head.

"For though from out our borne of time and place.

The flood may bear me far

I hope to meet my pilot face to face

When I have crossed the bar"

My part time assignments lasted until I developed Prostate Cancer. The work became too much for the body, even after surgery and radiation treatments.

I turned in my gear for good and called it quits May 2008.

Chapter XII

Night patrol on the Columbia, 2008 style.

After a nearly twenty year break from the Columbia River, I was eagerly anticipating the chance to accompany Oregon State Police Troopers on a gillnet patrol out of St. Helens where I live.

I had been bugging the Wildlife Captain to let me ride along and do a story on their patrols, just as we had taken reporters and writers on our patrols years ago.

Finally they called and invited me along!

The season was open for one 12 hour period in a restricted zone above the mouth of the Lewis River. I met up with Luke and Tim Schwartz, both Fish and Wildlife Troopers, Luke stationed at St. Helens, and Tim at Astoria. I had worked with both on contract fall Fish and Wildlife assignments in the past year. Both are highly trained, skillful operators, dedicated to their careers.

They launched the 26 foot specialized aluminum patrol boat and we ventured out into the river, immediately contacting a commercial gill netter coming in. Tim boarded the boat and checked the two men. They had already offloaded their catch, one Salmon, at a buy boat stationed at the lower deadline. They were done for the night.

We headed upstream observing a confusion of shore lights, navigation markers, anchored gillnet boats, drifting gillnet boats and ones that were running back upstream to repeat their downstream drift. The river here is wide and bordered on both sides with sandy beaches.

The current was running strong and some of the boats were obviously out of their home element. The way it usually works, a gillnet boat fishes home grounds when the season is wide open. They can lay out up to 1500 feet of net that then floats with the current. They are intimately familiar with the markers, obstructions, length of drifts and can literally operate in the dark.

Tonight however there were some operators from other areas that were closed, trying to get a successful drift in while being "corked' by the locals. High boats had 8-10 fish while lower boats had 4. Tim boarded one boat that had just finished a drift and was eager to get back to the top of the drift. Tim rode along while he maneuvered his gillnet boat back up and deftly laid out his net just a few feet below his competitor effectively ending his drift. The newcomer had no choice but to pull his gear and try to find an open area to lay out.

Upriver there were 10-15 boats all jockeying for position. Some were anchored, content to wait till the other had finished before trying their drift. Tim confidently jumped from the patrol boat to the gillnet boat decks with 3-4 feet of space, making and old war horse like me wince. These young Troopers are extremely confident in their skills and keep themselves in perfect physical condition.

After checking some 8-10 boats, all in compliance we decided to run downriver to check the closed area. I was pleased I still had my night vision despite my 67 years of age. I thought sure it would be gone like a lot of other things we tend to lose.

As we headed off downriver the low light clouds reflected much of the ground light back onto the river making it very easy to see the surface and far ahead.

Radar and GPS navigation screens made it that much easier. The boat performed flawlessly obviously designed and equipped with the latest electronic gadgetry. I immediately compared it mentally to the equipment we had suffered through. I recalled writing reports to the brass trying to justify such luxuries as trim tabs!

I recalled the old conservative attitudes of higher ups that surmised boats like cars were designed a certain way and add ons only detracted from their engineered designs.

I pointed out some of the old popular illegal gillnet sites near the Kalama River mouth. We continued downriver to the Cottonwood Island area. It was just another quiet night on the river with nothing amiss as far as we could see.

Tim took the wheel from Luke for the trip back upriver.

I thought to myself on the return trip what it must be like to be able to work alongside your own brother on a job like this, knowing he has the same training and skills you have. I used to marvel at my own good luck of landing a job that paid me to do things I loved.

Luke Schwartz has been honored by Shikar Safari Club for outstanding Fish and Wildlife work and also selected as Fish and Wildlife Officer of the year. Tim won't be far behind, I'm sure of that.

Tim expertly guided the 26 foot boat into the slip at St. Helens without so much as a bump on either side.

I gave them a copy of the recent Tide magazine with the article about past gillnet adventures. Both of them had things to take care of the next day. I knew all I had to do was go home and get some sleep.

The only downside I can see regarding river patrols is the fact that they have to work commercial seasons in the dark. There are few game officers in the area, in fact less than we had in the 80s and 90s. Priorities need to be established and legal fishing needs to be conducted in the light of day. I know gill netters bristle at the suggestion that illegal acts happen, but they do, and there has to be a better way.

There are too many hazards to consider while checking boats at night. The operator of the gillnet boat may not be aware of the position of the patrol boat. Boarding is a split second act and if one boat suddenly moves in another direction, stuff happens.

I also thought back to the long nights we spent with media in the boat and nothing happened. Then on solo patrols all hell would break loose. Kind of like the description of piloting an aircraft. Hours and hours of sheer boredom punctuated by seconds of sheer terror!

My hat goes off to the Fish and Wildlife Officers of Oregon State Police and Washington Department of Fish and Wildlife.

It's the kind of job you secretly know you would not trade for anything else, while most of the public would not have anything to do with it.

Commercial fishing at night may soon become a thing of the past. Night patrols will have to continue however. Poachers have always preferred to use darkness as cover.

Looking back on 20+ years on the river, countless contacts and adventures, I can't imagine having done anything else. To me it was the ultimate outdoor job and the river was my office. Many nights were uneventful. But I still recall the return trips upriver, after all night in the dark, the sun rising in the east and the river stretching out far ahead with Mt. Hood in the background.

Today almost all the old commercial fish stations are either falling into the river in decay or have been removed. Many of the gill net permits have been unused for years. Fishermen are being encouraged to experiment with more selective ways of catching fish.

Another way of life is slowly disappearing from the river. Whether the fish will recover and become again the mightiest run of salmon in the world remains to be seen.

I hope there continues to be a presence of law enforcement on the river. It requires a great deal of sacrifice, dedication and sheer love of being on the water.

It can be the greatest job in the world or it can be a boat ride!

Special tribute to the men that are no longer with us who worked the river and guided me along the way. I will never forget them!

Sgt. Henry Balensifer OSP

Sgt. Gary Suhadolnik WDFW

Sgt. Glen Tucker OSP

Sgt. Ken Moore OSP

Senior Trooper Russ Ellsworth OSP

Special Agent Rich Sievertson NMFS

11343159R00079

Made in the USA
Charleston, SC
17 February 2012